# Inferno
# Revealed

# Inferno Revealed

## FROM DANTE TO DAN BROWN

DEBORAH PARKER AND MARK PARKER

**palgrave**
**macmillan**

INFERNO REVEALED
Copyright © Deborah Parker and Mark Parker, 2013

First published in 2013 by PALGRAVE MACMILLAN® in the
U.S.—a division of St. Martin's Press LLC, 175 Fifth Avenue,
New York, NY 10010.

Where this book is distributed in the UK, Europe and the rest of
the world, this is by Palgrave Macmillan, a division of Macmillan Publishers Limited, registered in England, company number
785998, of Houndmills, Basingstoke, Hampshire RG21 6XS.

Palgrave Macmillan is the global academic imprint of the above
companies and has companies and representatives throughout
the world.

Palgrave® and Macmillan® are registered trademarks in the
United States, the United Kingdom, Europe and other countries.

ISBN: 978-1-137-27906-4

The Library of Congress has catalogued the hardcover edition
as follows:

Parker, Deborah, 1954– author.
    Inferno revealed : from Dante to Dan Brown / Deborah Parker
and Mark Parker.
        pages   cm
    ISBN 978-1-137-27906-4 (alk. paper)
    1. Dante Alighieri, 1265–1321. Inferno. 2. Dante Alighieri,
1265–1321—Influence. 3. Brown, Dan, 1964– Inferno. 4. Hell
in literature. I. Parker, Mark, 1956– author. II. Title.

PQ4380.P37   2013
851'.1—dc23
                                                        2013027567

A catalogue record of the book is available from the British
Library.

Design by Letra Libre

First edition: October 2013

10  9  8  7  6  5  4  3  2  1

Printed in the United States of America.

# Contents

# List of Figures

# Note to the Reader

All the quotations (except as noted) of Dante in this volume are from *The Divine Comedy*, translated with a commentary by Charles S. Singleton, Princeton University Press.

This book is directed to general readers. We hope *Inferno Revealed: From Dante to Dan Brown* will provide an engaging introduction to Dante's *Inferno* and the lively tradition of literary adaptations it has inspired.

# Introduction

It's no wonder that a shrewd popular writer like Dan Brown would choose the *Inferno,* the first book of Dante Alighieri's three-part *Divine Comedy,* as a point of departure for his latest novel. Great works of art often inspire later writers, but few poems have provided such fertile material for the creative energies of artists and writers as Dante's *Inferno.* And certain features of this masterpiece lend themselves especially well to adaptation and development.

Part of the poem's force lies in an unusual choice made by the author. Dante is writing a particular kind of poem, an epic, which has certain rules. For the most part Dante follows these conventions, but he swerves from them in one important way: He chose to make his epic *personal,* to put himself at the center of it. Unlike other epic poems, the *Inferno* puts unprecedented emphasis on what was near, even local, to the poet's experience.

This decision has consequences in the poem, and later writers have reaped the benefit of Dante's inspired turn from one of the familiar features of the epic. By making his particular experience central to the poem, Dante ensured that a certain tension would exist in the poem's deepest structure and that a certain level of mystery would surround his story. The *Inferno* is an old poem, and old poems often seem strange to modern readers. But the locality and particularity of the characters and places that Dante employs heightens the strangeness of the *Inferno.*

Like all epics, Dante's poem reaches from the depths of Hell to the stars, but along the way, it is filled with small-town rivalries, political rancor, bitter religious conflict, slander, and what sounds a lot like gossip.

Dan Brown gets a lot right about Dante in his *Inferno*. He understands the power of Dante's visual imagination, the magnificence and the intricacy of the Hell he creates. Like many other writers before him working in Dante's wake, Brown grasps the genius of Dante's connection of punishment with sin in the afterlife, the contrapasso. Further, he fully appreciates Dante's insistence on the relevance of the infernal journey to life on earth—the moral implications of an afterlife that so often reflects the corruption and crime of life on earth. Finally, Brown seizes upon an aspect of Dante's poem that recent writers have not exploited—the poem's combination of prophecy and savage indignation. His novel uses Dante's poem as a starting point in his own fiction. His Dante is a *version* of Dante. This book, *Inferno Revealed*, offers an account of why the *Inferno* is a great work of literature and why it has proven so inspirational to other writers. As we shall see, the two things needn't be connected: Great works of literature can be dead ends as well as spurs to invention for the writers who follow. But in the case of the *Inferno*, Dante combines these two literary functions.

Like many older poems, the *Inferno* can be hard for modern readers to understand. Its pleasures can seem a bit foreign. Often what goes without saying for Dante is something we don't know, and often his sense of what we might know—people, places, and things—is strange to us. If you want to read Dante, there are some things you need to know about the poet himself, his times, and epic poems in general.

Let's start by considering what epic poems like the *Inferno* do. A long narrative poem, an epic typically celebrates heroic actions by a larger-than-life protagonist. The style of such a poem is usually elevated, even lofty. Often such poems are ways of celebrating the founding of a people—like Virgil's *Aeneid,* which tells the story of the first Romans—or an important event in a culture—like Homer's *Iliad,* which retells the story of the Trojan War. In the largest sense, an epic tells a people where they came from, what their values are, why they should be proud of themselves, and possibly what destiny they might have as a people or nation.

While this is a workable description of an epic, we should keep in mind that the *Inferno* is more than this: It is also an acknowledged classic. In addition to knowing what kind of poem it is, we need to think a bit about what being a classic means. For that, we have to move from classifying the poem to thinking about what has happened to it over time. We need to think of what readers do with poems like this—that is, how they read the *Inferno,* and what kind of reputation it has earned.

This might seem an odd way of proceeding. But over the years, scholars have provided many accounts of how people read, and creative writers often tell their readers how they'd like their books to be read. These accounts range from extremely complicated models, which try to account for everything in the reading experience, to more rough-and-ready methods. We'd like to consider one of the latter. In thinking about what makes a classic, we want to focus on how a work of art can be used as a prompt to other creative acts and how it can be repurposed by readers to address problems or explore experiences that its author might not have intended.

More important, we want to emphasize one aspect of a classic: its adaptability or productivity. This approach focuses on the peculiar capacity of classic texts to suggest new meanings to other writers and new audiences. Here the emphasis is on the changes in human nature over time—more exactly, the audience's nature. Highly adaptable works have an uncanny ability to generate new readings, to take on a new life in different historical periods. Viewed this way, we might see a classic work like Dante's *Inferno* as constantly changing. This poem's adaptability is borne out by the extent and variety of reactions it has provoked over time. These reactions usually take the form of direct references to the poem in other literary texts—allusions, parodies, reuses of thematic material, imitations of Dante's style. Dante's *Divene Comedy,* particularly the *Inferno,* has generated many interpretations; the poem has meant different things to different readers in different places. It also has meant different things to different writers who have exploited its features in new ways.

It's one thing to acknowledge that a work is unusually suggestive or adaptable. We can demonstrate that easily by simply listing later works that return to it for inspiration. The more difficult question is to ask *why* certain works of literature prove so adaptable, why writers return to them again and again, and why subsequent reuses of these works seem so surprising and ultimately satisfying. Put another way, what did Dan Brown and others see in Dante's poem that prompted them to write?

We think that this is a mystery worth pursuing, and this book attempts to answer the questions posed by the *Inferno*'s influence on later writers. To do this, we've divided our book into two parts. The first explores one of the most original features of the *Inferno*—Dante's decision to make himself the hero of his own poem. By choosing to make his epic personal, Dante swerves from the lofty distance employed by other epic writers, who tell old stories whose elements are mythical or lost in the mists of time. Dante localizes his story, populating his Hell with contemporary Florentines, some of whom he knew intimately. The *Inferno* has supernatural and mythical elements, but again and again Dante brings to the forefront the world that he knew well. In chapters 1 through 5 we examine the consequences of this imaginative choice, which generates a tension in the poem between the timeless and the historically specific. We'll see how this choice ensures that readers of the poem will encounter a certain mystery about characters and events, ambiguities that prove both irresistible and suggestive.

Dante's personalization of the epic genre provides opportunities for later writers. In chapters 6 through 9 we show how subsequent writers have responded to and repurposed the *Inferno*. In tracing this process of response and adaptation, we look at both the high literary tradition as well as more popular uses of the poem. We conclude with a discussion of Dan Brown's use of Dante and an annotated list of every mention of the *Inferno* in the novel.

"Dante and Shakespeare divide the world between them," T. S. Eliot famously opined, "there is no third." While it is always dangerous to disagree with a critic of his acumen, we take another tack in this book. For it is not so much how Dante "divide[s] the world" as how his poem has expanded it that most interests us. The *Inferno* is not only creative in itself; it sparks creativity in others.

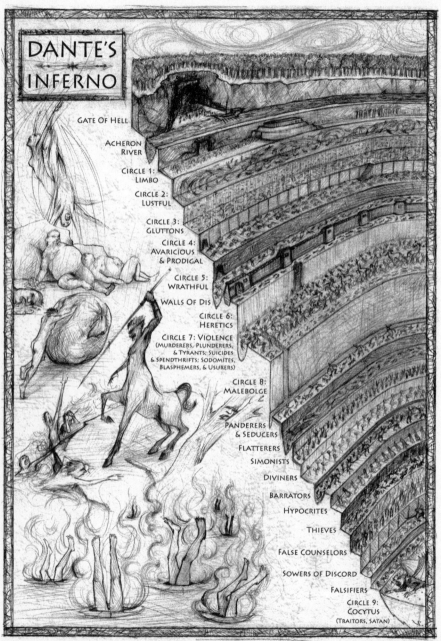

Fig. 1. Map of Hell

by Christian Paniagua

# 1

# Dante as Protagonist

## *How Making Yourself the Hero of Your Own Poem Changes Everything*

When Virgil wrote his epic, the *Aeneid*, he did so at a considerable distance from his subject. He was a court poet, a client of Augustus Caesar, and he wrote within a sophisticated political and cultural circle. The story he told, of Aeneas's flight from Troy and his founding of the Roman Empire, was both mythical and familiar to his contemporaries. His role was to put its loosely connected and contradictory elements into the most beautiful and memorable poetic form that his considerable talent could produce. Virgil does not appear in the poem, except to make brief pleas to his Muse to inspire him. The action of the heroic poem—the deeds of Aeneas—is hidden in the mist of time, and while it has clear relevance to Virgil's world, the connections are made across a temporal gulf.

Similarly, when John Milton began his epic, *Paradise Lost,* he undertook to tell the story of the rebellious angel Satan, the war in Heaven between God and Satan, the expulsion of Satan's army of fallen angels, and the temptation and fall of Adam and Eve in Eden. Milton sought to "justify the ways of God to men," but he did not see any reason to include himself in the story. Like Virgil, from time to time he asks for heavenly inspiration in his writing, and he tells us in no uncertain terms that his Muse dictates the poem to him at night. But he is not the protagonist any more than any other Christian is a protagonist in God's plan for the world. In taking this position as poet, both Virgil and Milton followed Homer, whose *Odyssey* and *Iliad* were the standards for the epic in Western culture. Homer is the singer of a tale, not the recounter of his own exploits.

Dante's poem could not be more different. Virgil, as he begins the *Aeneid,* sings "of arms and a man." Dante writes: "Midway in the journey of our life *I* found myself in a dark wood, for the straight way was lost" (*Inf.* 1.1–3; emphasis added). The prominence of the "I" here warrants notice. Dante is the protagonist, front and center in this epic. His story is, in ways far beyond Virgil's or Milton's poem, *his.* He does not simply recount; he is changed by the experience, finding a personal good in his journey, a journey that leads to salvation.

This swerve from epic tradition is bold enough, but Dante doubles down on this opening gambit. He complicates his presence in the poem by making a distinction between Dante the poet and Dante the pilgrim. One Dante narrates the story as a memory of a voyage through the afterlife. The other Dante, the pilgrim, has a different role in the story. He is the wayfarer or traveler, accompanied by his guide, Virgil, through Inferno and Purgatory.

The consequences for Dante's decision to put himself at the center of his epic are enormous, and they reverberate throughout the *Inferno*. Dante must project and characterize himself. In doing so, his personal attachments also become important; they are not petty details that vanish as he assumes the position of epic poet. One of the consequences of Dante's insistence on himself as pilgrim is that his temperament, personal entanglements, and ambitions become the raw material of the poem.

## THE DARK WOOD:
## DANTE'S MEETING WITH VIRGIL

The persistence and intensity of Dante's assertion of his own central role begins at once—in the first of the 34 cantos (divisions of the poem akin to chapters in a novel) of the *Inferno*, where Dante describes the conditions that give rise to his journey through the afterlife. Dante wanders in a "dark wood." He has lost the "straight way." Morally and physically exhausted, overcome by fear and sorrow, he compares his plight to that of a swimmer, one who has barely reached the shore, a man who has narrowly escaped death. Suddenly other elements come into play. He is no longer the lone figure in this landscape. We have movement from many directions: In rapid succession, a leopard, lion, and she-wolf assail him. The lean, ravenous wolf poses the greatest threat and causes the pilgrim to retreat into the wood "where the sun is silent" (*Inf.* 1.60)—that is, where there is no hope.

This is one of the most densely symbolic scenes in the poem. Many of the particulars have an allegorical significance. A Greek word, "allegory" means to speak figuratively of something else. In an allegory, entities have another meaning. In allegorical terms, Dante has strayed from the path of righteousness and truth and wanders in error and desperation. The allegorical significance of the wood and the three beasts derive from a number of traditions—literary, mystical, iconographic, and folk. For example, the association of a forest with sin and error derives from chivalric romances, in which questing knights would often get lost. The three beasts represent different sins— the leopard stands for lust, the lion, violence, and the she-wolf, avarice.

Up to this point in the poem, Dante's combination of allegory and personal presence still allows him to project himself as a kind of everyman. But Dante continues to raise the stakes. A lost soul needs a guide. A saint or angel might have done the trick, but the next section of canto 1 shows the consequences of Dante's decision to cast himself as the protagonist of his epic. After the she-wolf forces him back into the wood, the pilgrim utters "Miserere," a cry for help. No sooner than he emits this cry, Virgil comes to his aid. But Dante does not know yet the identity of the soul and asks him if he is a shade or a man.

> "No, not a living man, though once I was," he answered me,
> "and my parents were Lombards, both Mantuans by birth. I
> was born *sub Julio*, although late, and I lived at Rome under
> the good Augustus, in the time of the false and lying gods. I
> was a poet, and I sang of that just son of Anchises who came
> from Troy after proud Ilium was burned." (*Inf.* 1.67–75)

The way in which Virgil introduces himself and the way in which the pilgrim responds to him tell us much about how Dante regards Latin culture generally and Virgil in particular. Virgil, the eminent Latin poet, acquires a second life in Dante's Christian epic. The selection of Virgil, whose epic celebrates the founding of Roman civilization, informs the *Divine Comedy* in significant ways. First and foremost, we learn something about one of Dante's most profound attachments—his love of Virgil's work. Dante could have made the voyage himself, encountered allegorical personifications of sins, or chosen a religious figure for his guide. But he chose Virgil, an indication of his immense esteem for classical culture.

By choosing Virgil as guide, Dante gives an immediate complexity to his story. A Christian epic like the *Divine Comedy* doesn't obviously authorize such a choice—it might be more fitting to choose a saint, an angel, or at least a fellow Christian as a guide to salvation. The choice of Virgil introduces a certain tension into the *Inferno:* The journey to God is through or by way of a pagan and his pagan epic. Because of his profound personal connection with Virgil and classical culture, Dante's poetic avocation and ambition receive strong emphasis. The outsized presence of the classical past clashes with the providential narrative line and some of the poem's Christian assumptions.

Upon finding himself before his literary idol, Dante pays a heartfelt tribute to Virgil:

> "Are you, then, that Virgil, that fount which pours forth so broad a stream of speech?" I answered him, my brow covered with shame. "O glory and light of other poets, may the long study and the great love that have made me search your volume avail me! You are my master and my author. You alone are he from whom I took the fair style that has done me honor." (*Inf.* 1.79–87)

In these lines Dante reveals much about his love of Virgil's works. Dante refers to Virgil as a "fount," a life-giving generative force, and a "light," a beacon of inspiration not only for Dante but for countless other poets. Dante is a devoted follower of Virgil and has read his works with "long study" and "great love." He emulates the Latin poet's lofty epic style. Any honor that Dante has won for his literary achievements is owing to Virgil's illumination. When Virgil offers to guide Dante, the pilgrim readily accedes. Virgil will first guide him through Hell, an "eternal" place, after which they will see the souls in Purgatory. Then "a soul worthier than I," namely Beatrice, will take over as Dante's guide in Paradise.

This fervent speech deserves close attention. We see the tension between classical and Christian elements clearly, as Dante hails Virgil as "master and author" and thanks him for the fame he has achieved as poet. Worldly acclaim sits uneasily with the providential journey, just as Virgil, a damned soul, seems an eccentric choice of guide. Virgil will lead Dante through Purgatory, a region that is forbidden to him. One might explain Virgil's presence by recalling the attempt in early Christian culture to reclaim the poet as an unconscious prophet of Christianity. One of Virgil's poems, the *Fourth Eclogue,* concerns the birth of a miraculous child, and church commentators often read it as a premonition of Christ's birth. But such attempts at rehabilitation do not make pagan and Christian culture agree; they simply testify to the force of a desire to remove contradiction.

The first canto ends with Dante declaring his readiness to follow Virgil. In the second canto, Dante starts second-guessing himself and hesitates. Apprehensive about his worthiness to embark on such a journey, he tells Virgil, "But I, why do I come there? And who allows it? I am not Aeneas, I am not Paul; of this neither I nor others think me worthy" (*Inf.* 2.31–33). The allusion to Aeneas and Paul is highly significant, as both undertook trips to the afterlife. Aeneas travels to the underworld in order to speak with the shade of his father, Anchises, who foretells the glorious achievements of his son's descendants. Aeneas is nothing less than the progenitor of the Roman Empire, the one "chosen as father of glorious Rome and of her empire."

The purpose of St. Paul's journey is no less momentous. Paul, the "Chosen Vessel," was rapt to the third heaven by God. Paul, originally named Saul, was an unbeliever and persecutor of Christians before his conversion. While on the road to Damascus, he was struck blind by God and subsequently underwent a dramatic conversion. After he was blinded, Paul possessed far greater vision. His trip to Heaven also had a providential purpose—to bring confirmation of Truth, God, and faith to others.

These two precedents—Aeneas and Paul—provide an important perspective on Dante's status as epic hero. In linking himself to Aeneas and Paul, Dante emphasizes the importance of his voyage—and his worthiness to undertake it. This moment of alignment with Aeneas and Paul stands as an index of Dante's bold swerve from epic conventions. If Dante is not worthy of being elevated to the status of epic protagonist, neither are the contemporaries who populate his afterlife. If Dante is neither Aeneas nor Paul, Francesca isn't a Cleopatra or Paolo a Tristan.

## BEATRICE

Dante takes pains to show that his voyage, like those of Aeneas and Paul, is divinely sanctioned. Virgil assures the pilgrim of this by recounting the story of Beatrice's visit to him in Limbo (the first of Hell's nine circles). Beatrice is the most significant local feature of Dante's *Divine Comedy*. To understand her intervention, we need to look at the backstory of Dante's beloved. Although we do not know exactly who the historical Beatrice was, Dante's son Piero, who wrote a commentary to the poem, identified her as Beatrice Portinari. Giovanni Boccaccio, author of the *Decameron* and the first biography of Dante, further reports that she was the daughter of Folco Portinari, a Florentine banker. Dante first writes of Beatrice in an earlier work, the *Vita Nuova* (*New Life*), which examines his infatuation with her. The work mixes spiritual exaltation and religious transformation with an intense eroticism by combining the fiercest intellectual rigor in tracing the significance of his love with a lush romanticism in describing pivotal moments of the relationship.

Dante first encountered Beatrice when he was nine and she was eight; he saw her again nine years later. What we know about this relationship comes almost entirely from Dante's account of it in the *Vita Nuova,* which idealizes and poeticizes it. Since women of Beatrice's class were sequestered until marriage, each meeting was momentous for Dante. The encounters themselves—more precisely these sightings or greetings—would have been facilitated by the proximity of their homes. Dante's Florence was divided into six subdivisions known as *sesti,* or sixths. The Alighieri lived in the sesto of San Pier Scheraggi and the Portinari in that of San Pier Maggiore. The houses of the two families might have been as little as 50 yards apart. In any case, Dante's Beatrice, if not the proverbial girl next door, was the girl in the next sixth. In the *Divine Comedy,* she is Dante's inspiration and spiritual guide. Beatrice embodies absolute perfection and functions as an intermediary in Dante's ascent to God.

Without Beatrice, Dante's *Divine Comedy* would not exist; Beatrice, as we learn, sets the voyage in motion. Virgil makes this explicit when he tells Dante of her visit to Virgil in Limbo. The lines that describe Beatrice's appearance are among the most beautiful in the *Inferno.* "Her eyes were more resplendent than the stars, and she began to say to me, sweetly and softly, in an angelic voice . . ." (*Inf.* 2.55–57). To describe Beatrice's divine beauty and grace, Dante draws on the style of writing he had used in the *Vita Nuova.* This poetic style, called the Dolce Stil Novo (Sweet New Style), refers to Italian courtly poetry of the thirteenth century: The terms "sweet" and "new" refer to both the words and the melodic, lyrical style of the poetry itself. To emphasize these associations between Beatrice and the Dolce Stil Novo, Dante laces these lines describing his beloved with expressions that recall this kind of writing, such as "*stella*" (star), "*dir soave e piana*" (say to me . . . softly), and "*angelica voce*" (angelic voice). Dante will use this style again when he encounters Beatrice at the top of Purgatory.

Just as Dante elevates himself in aligning himself with Aeneas and Paul, so does he elevate his beloved. Describing the scene in Heaven that preceded her visit to Virgil in Limbo, Beatrice informs the Roman poet that St. Lucy, a fourth-century martyr of Syracuse and the patron saint of sight, had alerted her to Dante's distress in the dark wood. Another blessed woman, the Virgin Mary, had summoned Lucy, forming a chain of concerned women who intercede for Dante. Thus we see that Dante's love, Beatrice, becomes the "local" presence among three blessed heavenly women. The sanction for his voyage could hardly have come from a higher authority, but the mediation ends with a contemporary person.

Ultimately, Dante's double selection of guides creates an oscillation in the poem. He projects a range of affiliation that cannot form a continuum: The classical and the Christian cannot easily coexist. Again Dante complicates his journey to God by including other elements.

## DANTE AND THE CLASSICAL TRADITION

We can see some of this tension in Dante's next encounter. The pilgrim has just presented himself as the object of Christian intercession by three blessed women in Heaven and as a devotee of Virgil. This humility does not last for long. Upon entering the first circle of Hell, Dante meets the virtuous pagans, among them eminent poets, philosophers, and scientists. Here he meets the greatest poets of antiquity: Homer, author of the *Iliad* and *Odyssey;* Lucan, author of the *Pharsalia,* an account of the civil war between Roman Republicans and Julius Caesar; Horace, whose works include four books of Odes, the *Satires,* and the *Art of Poetry;* and Ovid, author of the *Metamorphoses.* This encounter provides the occasion for one of the most extraordinary moments in the poem. As Dante recollects, the six poets turn to him: "After they had talked awhile together, they turned to me with sign of salutation, at which my master smiled; and far more honor still they showed me, for they made me one of their company, so that I was sixth amid so much wisdom" (*Inf.* 4.97–102).

After a brief confabulation, the poets invite Dante to join their ranks. Through this maneuver, Dante presents himself the equal of Virgil, Homer, Ovid, Lucan, and Horace. They welcome Dante as one of their own *before* he has even written the *Divine Comedy*. It is as if one of our contemporary poets had staged his glorification by Shakespeare, Milton, and Spenser. Or as if Dan Brown had depicted a séance in which Edgar Allan Poe, Dashiell Hammett, and Arthur Conan Doyle honored him as one of the greatest of mystery writers. At this point in his career, Dante had written some lyric poems and the *New Life*. One might say that he's writing a check with these words that he hasn't earned enough reputation to cash. But this episode isn't simply the record of Dante's presumption. It sits uneasily against the previous discussion of the three women. Dante basks in secular poetic honor immediately after he professes himself humbled by the action of Christian grace—the intercession of Mary, St. Lucy, and Beatrice. Pride as poet—even if it is deserved—sits awkwardly with the passage of the grace-filled soul to salvation.

## DANTE CHALLENGES OVID AND LUCAN

Dante is not shy about his aspirations as poet. If in Limbo Dante congratulates himself on an eminence that he has not yet achieved, in the cantos of the thieves (*Inf.* 24 and 25) he aspires to earn this reputation through a bit of virtuoso writing. The requirements of the poem, as he has conceived it, require that he describe the punishment of the thieves, their spectacular transformation, and concomitant loss of identity. This is the justness of their punishment: Those who stole from others now have their identities, their very beings, stolen from them.

Like Indiana Jones looking into one of the tombs in *Raiders of the Lost Ark*, Dante, gazing into the pit containing the thieves, is horrified by swarms of snakes and reptiles:

> Amid this cruel and most dismal swarm were people running naked and terrified, without hope of hiding-place or heliotrope. They had their hands bound behind with serpents: these thrust through their loins the head and tail, which were knotted in front.
>
> And lo! at one who was near our bank darted a serpent that transfixed him there where the neck is joined to the shoulders . . . (*Inf.* 24.91–99)

Snakes and serpentine creatures carry out a variety of intimate assaults on the thieves. They wind themselves tightly around their bodies, bind them stealthily, and then bite them savagely. The effect is surprising and spectacular. Once bitten, the soul incinerates instantly then rises again utterly bewildered. No less chilling is the speed with which this process takes place—in the brief time it takes to write the letter "o" or "i."

Nor does Dante simply narrate these changes. In the next canto he enters into a kind of contest with earlier poets, boisterously vying with them in feats of poetic bravura. Before challenging other poets directly, however, he provides the reader with more evidence of his capabilities. Raising his finger from his chin to his nose, he gestures to Virgil to remain alert.

Peering into the pit, he sees three Florentine thieves arrive on the scene looking for one of their comrades. They do not realize that he is nowhere to be found because he has been transformed into a serpent. A lizard darts by and bites one of the thieves. As a horrifying fusion between man and reptile takes place, the other two souls stare transfixed. Dante the pilgrim is confounded as well:

> While I kept my eyes on them, lo! a serpent with six feet darts up in front of one and fastens on him all over. With the middle feet it clasped the belly, and with its fore feet took his arms, then struck his teeth in one and the other cheek; its hind feet it spread upon his thighs, and put its tail between them, and bent it upwards on his loins behind. Ivy was never so rooted to a tree as the horrid beast entwined its own limbs round the other's; then, as if they had been of hot wax, they stuck together and mixed their colors, and neither the one nor the other now seemed what it was at first: even as in advance of the flame a dark color moves across the paper, which is not yet black and the white dies away. The other two were looking on, and each cried, "Oh me, Agnello, how you change! Lo, you are already neither two nor one!"
>
> Now the two heads had become one, when we saw the two shapes mixed in one face, where both were lost. Two arms were made of the four lengths; the thighs with the legs, the belly and the chest, became members that were never seen before. Each former feature was blotted out: the perverse image seemed both and neither, and such, with slow pace, it moved away. (*Inf.* 25.49–78)

In these lines Dante describes the unimaginable: Agnello, one of the thieves, and a lizard gradually merge into one into one grotesque, hybrid monster. As in his comparison of the speed with which the thieves are incinerated and resurrected to the mundane activity of writing letters, so Dante draws here on the ordinary to describe the extraordinary. To convey the tightness with which the serpent winds its six legs across Agnello's body, Dante compares it to ivy clinging to a vine. As serpent and thief become one monstrosity, obliterating the features of each, he compares the process to melting wax. As one of the thieves observes, this new monster is neither two nor one—neither snake nor man.

Few passages in literature can match this display of vivacity and invention. The comparisons function brilliantly, enabling readers to visualize a mesmerizing transformation. The passage exemplifies T. S. Eliot's observation in a 1929 essay simply titled "Dante" about Dante's greatness as a poet—that he excels in creating "clear visual images." It's hard to imagine a more exact and arresting image than Dante's attempt to convey the intermediate state of the transformation: the uneven movement of the discoloration, the flaring and sputtering flame, the impossibility of saying whether a spot is now burned (black) or yet untouched (white).

At moments like this, the journey to salvation seems to fade in importance, as the pleasures of virtuoso writing become prominent. Such a passage is less about salvation than about poetic ambition—less about Dante the pilgrim as an everyman on an arduous climb to Heaven than Dante the poet flexing his creative muscles.

Before describing another awesome transformation, Dante boasts of his prowess. No poet has described, as Dante does now, a simultaneous double process of transformation:

> Let Lucan now be silent, where he tells of the wretched Sabellus and of Nasidius, and let him wait to hear what now comes forth. Concerning Cadmus and Arethusa let Ovid be silent, for if he, poetizing, converts the one into a serpent and the other into a fountain, I envy him not; for two natures front to front he never so transmuted that both forms were prompt to exchange their substance. (*Inf.* 25.94–102)

And in fact, by comparison to Dante's descriptions, Lucan's and Ovid's descriptions of transformation, while formidable, seem less precise and less powerful. Sabellus and Nasidius were soldiers in Cato's army in Lucan's *Pharsalia*. After a snake bites him, Sabellus's body melts into a pool. After another snake poisons Nasidius, his body swells into a globe and bursts his armor. In Ovid's *Metamorphoses,* Cadmus (the legendary founder of Troy) is transformed into a serpent, but the poet does not enter into the particularities of the metamorphosis. The goddess Diana changes Arethusa into a fountain when she answers the nymph's prayer for help as she is being pursued by the river god Alpheus. Dante declares that Ovid never described in such dramatic detail the exchanging of two natures. There's insolence to Dante's claim but also a sense in which he revels in his capacity as poet. His dazzling sample of his prowess does entitle him to the kind of honor that he associates with the poets he had encountered in Limbo. Although his earlier self-congratulation rang hollow in Limbo, his boasts now seem justified by the poem.

The second transformation describes a shade and reptile exchanging natures: The shade becomes a snake, the snake, a shade. The process begins with a lizard attacking and biting one of the thieves.

> They mutually responded in such a way that the reptile cleft its tail into a fork, and the wounded one drew his feet together. The legs and thighs so stuck together that soon no mark of the juncture could be seen; the cloven tail took on the shape that was lost in the other; and its skin grew soft, the other's hard. I saw the arms drawing in at the armpits, and the brute's two feet, which were short, lengthening out in proportion as the other's arms were shortening. Then the hind paws, twisted together, became the member that man conceals, and from his the wretch had put forth two feet. While the smoke veils the one and the other with a new color, and generates hair on the one part and strips it from the other, the one rose upright and the other fell down, but neither turned

aside the baleful lamps beneath which each was changing his muzzle. He that was erect drew his in toward the temples, and from the excess of matter that came in there the ears issued from the smooth cheeks; that which did not run back, but was retained, made of that excess a nose for the face and thickened the lips to due size. He that lay prone drives the snout forward and draws the ears back into the head as the snail does its horns; and the tongue, which before was whole and fit for speech, divides, and in the other the forked tongue joins up; and the smoke stops. (*Inf.* 25.103–138)

Dante has talked a great deal of talk in the poem—but now he walks the walk. We have much to admire here. In this second transformation, we witness the gradual, synchronized, reciprocal transformation of two natures as Agnello and a lizard exchange natures in a double process. It begins with the lizard biting Buoso in the navel, "that part by which we first receive our nourishment." Stunned, Buoso yawns as if taken over by sleep or fever. Dante successively describes each entity taking on the qualities of the other: The thief acquiring the reptilian skin of the serpent (and vice versa), the changes in their respective skins, the acquisition and loss of hair, the growth and disappearance of limbs, all happening as each stares into the eyes of the other. As thief and lizard glare at one another, both emit smoke—the man from his navel, the serpent from its mouth. The speed of the metamorphoses is also stunning. Among the fascinating details of the transformation are the puffs of smoke emitted from the serpent's mouth and from the wounds it inflicts, the locked stares of the entwined snake and sinner, and the inevitability of their fates.

## DANTE'S PRIDE

In the cantos of the thieves, Dante vies with his classical forbears. Later, in Purgatory, he turns to his contemporary competitors.

On the terrace of pride, Dante encounters Oderisi da Gubbio, a thirteenth century illuminator of manuscripts. The proud are hunched over: A heavy boulder weighs down each of the souls. Dante must bend over to speak to Oderisi. In life proud of his art, here a much humbler Oderisi tells Dante about the transitory nature of fame. Franco Bolognese has surpassed him just as the painter Giotto has surpassed Cimabue. The same thing has happened in the field of poetry.

> So has the one Guido taken from the other the glory of our tongue—and he perchance is born that shall chase the one and the other from the nest. Earthly fame is naught but a breath of wind, which comes hence and now comes thence, changing its name because it changes quarter. (Purg. 11.97–102)

The first Guido is generally understood to be a reference to Guido Guinizzelli, one of the most illustrious lyric poets of the previous generation and widely deemed father of the Sweet New School of poetry; the second to Guido Cavalcanti, another lyric poet and one of Dante's best friends before his exile. Cavalcanti has surpassed Guinizzelli. Moreover, Dante hints, someone is born whose work will surpass both these poets—so "he perchance is born that shall chase the one and the other from the nest." Most readers reasonably take this "he" to be a reference to Dante himself. Once again Dante displays his pride, but the context differs from what we saw in the cantos of the thieves. Although it is the nature of the artistic tradition to breed excellence, here artistic striving is shown to be a vanity. The lines imply that someone will inevitably surpass the one who once surpassed Cavalcanti and Guinizzelli. Dante's fame is doomed to be lost. In *Purgatory*, Dante looks at fame from a more lofty perspective and acknowledges the transitory nature of success. It makes no difference if one dies an old man or an infant; the duration of any person's fame is but a drop in the bucket of eternity.

Yet, in spite of such reservations about the ultimate worth and endurance of fame and about its fleeting nature, Dante does seek renown. When Beatrice visits Virgil in Limbo, she tells him that his fame "shall last as long as the world" (*Inf.* 2.59–60). These words suggest a very different take on fame from Odersi's words. They imply that nothing can diminish the greatness of some works. In bending over to speak to the proud, Dante participates symbolically in the expiation of this sin. By contrast, among the envious in Purgatory, the pilgrim declares that he will not be spending any time on this terrace— presumably because there is no one Dante envies.

There is a difference between pride and vanity. Pride concerns our estimation of ourselves, and it might well be warranted. Vanity, which concerns what others think of us, is far less justifiable. None of Dante's confidence in his poetic ability is unmerited, and, writing in the classical tradition, his assurance is hardly remarkable. The Roman poet Horace, in the final poem of the third book of his *Odes,* was not shy about his achievement. "I have completed an imperishable monument," he writes, and, moving from space to time, he adds that his name will be known so long as Rome stands. But insofar as the *Divine Comedy* is a Christian epic, a vision of the providential journey of the grace-filled soul to Heaven, it recommends other virtues, prominent among them humility. By making himself the hero of his epic, Dante generates a volatile mix of personal elements that are difficult to integrate into a providential structure.

This mix of elements has consequences for the tradition of writing that Dante so profoundly transforms. His triumph lies in his ability to fuse and partially reconcile antithetical elements in his poem. Like Horace, he creates an "imperishable monument," but he also inaugurates a live tradition for later writers. His example opens new prospects and new opportunities for those writing after him. Dante's poem is a durable monument—a masterpiece—but it is also a surprisingly useful template for further exploration of the human condition.

# 2

## Scandalous Contemporaries

*Dante's People*

There are people in every epic poem. What's remarkable about the *Divine Comedy* is the way Dante brings a new category of people to prominence. In the *Aeneid,* for instance, Virgil talks about mythological gods, such as Venus, or figures like Aeneas and Dido, who flicker between history and myth. Dante's epic includes such persons as well, but, for the most part, people in the *Inferno* tend to be contemporary historical Italians. Although Dante's contemporaries and subsequent readers would know figures such as Virgil and Cleopatra, people such as the glutton Ciacco (*Inf.* 6) or the counterfeiter Master Adam (*Inf.* 30) were not well known, and they are mysteries to modern readers. This use of contemporaneous characters creates interpretive problems for readers and scholars, since it has proven difficult or impossible to recover information on some figures. But it also reshapes epic conventions profoundly. In a sense, Dante doubles down with each new swerve from convention: He makes himself the hero of his epic, and, as a consequence, he reorients the world of the epic by drawing his contemporaries and near contemporaries into roles previously filled by mythological figures or revered historical personages.

This reorientation concerns not only what characters appear in the poem but also what the characters do. In the *Aeneid*, when the hero descends into the underworld to learn his future, it is delivered by authoritative figures, such as his father, Anchises, an estimable figure of myth in his own right. Other mythological figures, such as Deiphobus, fill Aeneas in on recent events. In each case, commanding personages deliver prophecy and make pronouncements on history. By contrast, Dante often puts prophecy and history into the mouths of far less exalted figures—even largely unknown ones. Moreover, Dante's people often go beyond predicting and reporting events. Instead of simply talking about what happened or what will happen, these characters address the why and the how of contemporary history. Dante's decision to include and emphasize people from his own time is one of the most original features of the *Divine Comedy*.

## THE NEUTRALS

Dante's swerve from epic conventions about character is made more striking by his presentation. Let's consider how the poet handles historical characters by taking a closer look at the pilgrim's encounters with people in the first eight cantos of the *Inferno*. Although this summary does not by any means exhaust the meetings with Italians, it allows us to see the effects of their inclusion and to gauge the importance of locals in this poem. The beginning of the *Inferno* follows the traditions of the epic fairly closely. In the first canto, Dante the pilgrim meets his guide, the Roman poet Virgil. After passing through the Gate of Hell at the beginning of *Inferno* 3, Dante sees the neutrals, indecisive cowardly souls who were so weak-minded in life that they do not even merit a place in Hell proper. He relegates them to the vestibule of Hell, the entrance area just inside the gate. The neutrals appear as a group, chasing a banner as swarms of insects sting them mercilessly. Tears stream down their bodies to gather in putrid puddles swirling with worms.

Although Dante recognizes one individual among the neutrals, he does not mention his name but identifies him as the shade "who from cowardice made the great refusal" (*Inf.* 3.60). Early commentators identified the shade as Pope Celestine V. It's sufficient to note here that although Dante doesn't mention a name, his readers generally understood that the poet refers here to a contemporary figure, and they began to solve the mysteries created by Dante's decision to focus on persons from his own era.

As Dante and Virgil approach the Acheron River in the third canto and see Charon, classical ferryman of the dead, we are still in the realm of familiar epic conventions. Charon is but the first of a number of infernal demons who seek to block the wayfarers' advance. Virgil dispenses with Charon's order that they back off, just as he handily dismisses efforts by other creatures to block their advance.[1] At the shores of the Acheron, Dante sees the suffering of recently damned souls. They howl in desperation, cursing God, their parents, and the day they were born. But he does not speak to anyone.

Upon entering the first circle of Hell, or Limbo, Dante encounters the great poets and philosophers of antiquity and the early Middle Ages. Although Dante imbues some of these virtuous pagans with a distinguishing characteristic, he presents them in groups. With the exception of Dante's meeting with Virgil in the first canto, up to this point we have not had an encounter with an individual. In this first stage of the journey, Dante presents Hell's inhabitants more as examples of certain qualities than as fully realized individuals.

## DANTE'S MEETING WITH FRANCESCA DA RIMINI

This pattern changes dramatically when Dante and Virgil enter the second circle of Hell. In this and the next three circles, all of Dante's exchanges are with contemporary Italians. Although he might note the presence of people from antiquity, he talks with figures from his own time. They include Francesca da Rimini among the lustful, the glutton Ciacco, and the wrathful Filippo Argenti. Dante characterizes these three figures in strikingly different ways. Looking at each meeting closely will allow us to see how he brings these figures to life.

In the second circle of Hell, Dante meets Francesca da Rimini. She captivates Dante, just as she has captivated readers of the poem for centuries. We can see the dramatic tension to come in the pilgrim's vivid description of her punishment:

> I came into a place mute of all light, which bellows like the sea in tempest when it is assailed by warring winds. The hellish hurricane, never resting, sweeps along the spirits with its rapine; whirling and smiting, it torments them. (*Inf.* 5.28–33)

The *contrapasso*, Dante's term for "counterpenalty"—the notion that the punishment should fit the crime—is clear. The lustful subjected "reason to desire" (*Inf.* 5.39). Just as their passions swept them up in life, so do the infernal winds batter them in Hell. As Dante and Virgil gaze on the thousands of souls flying about them, Virgil identifies some of the most famous lovers of antiquity by name: Semiramìs, Queen of Assyria, alleged to have legalized incest so she could have sex with her son; Cleopatra, Queen of Egypt and lover of Julius Caesar and Mark Antony; Helen of Troy, wife of Menelaus, King of Sparta, whose abduction by Paris initiated the Trojan War; the great Greek warrior Achilles; Paris, the Trojan prince who abducted Helen; and Tristan, the lover of Isolde, wife of King Mark in the French Breton romances. One would expect Dante the pilgrim to be greatly interested in hearing the stories of any one of them.

But Dante the poet upsets our expectations. Out of this dazzling array of famous lovers, Dante prefers to speak to the two "that go together" (*Inf.* 5.74), Paolo Malatesta and Francesca da Rimini. A noblewoman, Francesca was the wife of Gianciotto Malatesta, the lord of Rimini, a town on the Adriatic coast of Italy. Paolo was Gianciotto's brother. The historical record is murky, but according to some contemporary accounts, Paolo wooed Francesca as Gianciotto's proxy. Perhaps this is how they became lovers. Upon discovering her infidelity, Gianciotto brutally murdered them in 1282 or 1283. Years later, Francesca's nephew, Guido Novello da Polenta, offered Dante refuge during his exile. Dante likely learned something of their affair during his stay in Rimini. Presumably the story did not come to Dante with the lush romanticism of the Tristan myth or the moralistic sermonizing of the historical affair between Antony and Cleopatra. Unlike stories from the classical or romance traditions, Francesca's sensational infidelity and murder (and the accompanying fratricide) are relatively fresh— if not ripped from the headlines, then gleaned from local gossip.

The importance of the inclusion of two contemporaries here cannot be overestimated. This stunning move reorients Dante's epic in a singular way. Unlike Virgil, Dante does not want to tell the stories solely of people from antiquity. The pilgrim wants to hear the stories of people from his own time. The poet creates his own heroes and heroines or, in the case of the damned, his own gallery of fallen souls, and draws his own conclusions about them. In so doing, the state of his own world becomes one of the central topics of the poem. Such a move allows Dante to assess his own moment and analyze the factors contributing to its degeneration.

Although Paolo and Francesca move together, Francesca speaks on behalf of the couple. When she assumes center stage, her account of the overpowering effects of love holds readers spellbound.

> Love, which is quickly kindled in a gentle heart, seized this one for the fair form that was taken from me—and the way of it afflicts me still. Love, which absolves no loved one from loving, seized me so strongly with delight in him, that, as you see, it does not leave me even now. Love brought us to one death. Caina awaits him who quenched our life. (*Inf.* 5.100–107)

We now see how Dante makes his characters come alive, how he imbues them with qualities that turn them into literary legends in their own right. With her emphatic and incantatory repetition of the word "love" at the beginning of three successive tercets, Francesca identifies herself with desire. Presenting herself as a chivalric heroine, she underscores the overpowering effects of love and the extent to which she considers herself driven by it. Moreover, even in Hell, her love is fresh and vital. While Francesca abides her eternal punishment, she underscores the depth of her attachment.

Francesca stresses the overweening force of love further when she claims "Love, which absolves no loved one from loving." Again Dante emphasizes the irresistibility of love. It compels reciprocation. This dictum is not only an axiom of courtly love but a psychological truth: It's hard to dislike someone who likes you. Other details and admissions emerge, such as the couple's mutual physical attraction. Her "fair form" attracts Paolo just as his beauty captivates her. However, love is not the

Fig. 2. Gustave Doré, *Dante's Swoon,* Courtesy of the Division of Rare and Manuscript Collections, Cornell University Library.

only sentiment she feels: She also desires revenge—the manner of her death "afflicts" her. In the last line of the third tercet, she relegates Gianciotto, her murderer, to Caina, the ninth and lowest circle of Hell.

Overwhelmed by her words, Dante asks Francesca to reveal the roots of her passion. She responds by recalling the day she and Paolo were reading the story of Lancelot and Guinevere,

King Arthur's wife. When the two read that Lancelot kissed Guinevere, Paolo kissed Francesca. She sums up the fatal result of that kiss in the words "that day we read no farther." This gracious noblewoman retains her aristocratic bearing even in Hell. She is tactfully circumspect in her account of the momentous event that led to her damnation. Her story shatters Dante—and his readers. No stranger to love himself, the pilgrim swoons at the end of the canto.

Dante might well have assigned Lancelot and Guinevere to the circle, and he could have interviewed them. But they appear as elements of Francesca's story, not as characters in Dante's poem. Dante prefers to elevate a contemporary woman and her lover, who in telling their own story refer to a pair of the great adulterers in the courtly tradition.

## THE DAMNED AND PROPHECY: CIACCO ON THE FUTURE OF FLORENCE

Dante's meetings with the next two sinners, the glutton Ciacco and the wrathful Filippo Argenti, show the extent of his determination to localize the epic. Although each figure serves to exemplify the sins of circles 3 and 5, we also see how this practice tends to create puzzles and to provide opportunities for writers following Dante to address their own time and place. The identity of the historical Ciacco is unknown. While we have some knowledge of Francesca (her status as a noblewoman and the wife of the lord of Rimini give her some visibility), no details about Ciacco survive. Although we have no particular reason to doubt Ciacco's existence, Dante's use of little-known contemporaries like him introduces a certain element of mystery into the poem.

Ciacco recognizes Dante, but it is never clear if Dante recognizes him. (The filthy precipitation doesn't help matters.) But this uncertainty does not make the pilgrim less eager to question him about the future. Although Dante pities Ciacco, he plies him for information about their native city. In Homer's poem, when Odysseus seeks knowledge of the future, he speaks with Tiresias, the famous seer of myth. When Aeneas enters the underworld on a similar journey in the *Aeneid,* he speaks to characters met earlier in the story (his helmsman Palinurus) or renowned mythic figures (the silent but majestically expressive Dido or his father, Anchises). There is a certain logic to such choices. We do not know, however, why Dante chose a glutton to provide the first substantial discussion of Florentine politics in the poem, although this element of the presentation might have been important in itself.

Ciacco was a rather common name in Dante's time—often a nickname for Jacopo. The name also implies "pig" or "hog." Unlike the majority of historical characters in the *Divine Comedy,* Ciacco is not a nobleman but rather a member of the merchant or middle class. What little we know about Ciacco comes from the work of a later writer, Giovanni Boccaccio, who includes a story about the glutton in his *Decameron* (written between 1351 and 1353). According to Boccaccio's story, Ciacco was a wit and a parasite, an inveterate freeloader who popped up at the homes of wealthy families at mealtimes. In exchange for a meal, he would relay gossip and tell stories. In the absence of any supporting evidence about the historical Ciacco, Boccaccio's amusing little tales might well be considered a playful fabrication, an embellishment consistent with Dante's poem. More significantly, Boccaccio's story becomes one of a long line of additions, one of the first instances of adaptation of a particular detail from Dante's work. Setting the stage for later writers, Boccaccio exploits Dante's choice to use contemporary characters and offers his own lively take on Ciacco. Dante provides later writers with ample opportunities for creative adaptation.

Dante doesn't recognize Ciacco when the two meet. The filthy rain, snow, and gigantic hailstones that pour down on the gluttons make it impossible to distinguish anyone through the muck: "huge hail, foul water, and snow pour down through the murky air; the ground that receives it stinks. Cerberus, monstrous beast and cruel, with three throats barks doglike over the people who are here submerged" (*Inf.* 6.10–15).

As in many instances in the *Divine Comedy,* the art here lies in an implicit contrast between the circumstances of the sin itself and the punishment. Gluttony conjures up the pleasures of eating—often convivial, communal, or at least consoling. (The idea of "comfort food" is an enduring one.) We might even invoke another of Dante's works, the *Convivio,* or "Banquet," in which the exchange of philosophical ideas is likened—favorably—to the social pleasures of the table. In Hell, however, such niceties are exchanged for a sodden and solitary anonymity. The ground upon which the gluttons lie is putrid and muddy. The three-headed dog, Cerberus, torments the damned further, howling thunderously and mauling them. The eternal hail, snow, and wet reduce the gluttons to a bestial state: They bay like hounds in the rain.

As Dante and Virgil walk through this slough of supine souls, Ciacco, recognizing Dante, sits up to address him: "'O you that are led through this Hell,' he said to me, 'recognize me if you can: you were made before I was unmade'" (*Inf.* 6.40–42). Dante's contemporary explicitly calls to him as a contemporary—the poet was born before Ciacco died—and, in the next few lines, as a fellow Florentine. But the reference to Florence produces anxieties. Ciacco doesn't mention Florence by name but designates it as a "sack" overflowing with envy. The glutton's suffering overwhelms the pilgrim, who weeps upon learning of Ciacco's wretchedness. The pilgrim quickly switches gears, however, and changes the topic swiftly to politics:

> I answered him, "Ciacco, your misery so weighs upon me
> that it bids me weep. But tell me, if you can, what the citizens

of the divided city will come to; and if any one in it is just;
and tell me why such discord has assailed it." (*Inf.* 6.58–63)

Ciacco, like all the damned souls in the *Inferno*, has knowledge,
albeit limited, of future events. Dante takes advantage of this
knowledge and queries the glutton about the future of Florence.
Here another order of mystery enters the poem—puzzles that
Dante himself authorizes. The pilgrim asks Ciacco three questions: (1) What will become of Florence? (2) Are there any just
persons residing in the city? (3) What is the cause of all the civic
discord? Ciacco answers in the order in which the questions are
posed. His responses assume the form of a prophecy.

> After long convention they will come to blood, and the rus-
> tic party will drive out the other with much offense. Then,
> through the power of one who presently is temporizing, that
> party is destined to fall within three years, and the other to
> prevail, long holding its head high and keeping the other
> under heavy burdens, however it may lament and feel the
> shame. Two men are just, and are not heeded there. Pride,
> envy, and avarice are the three sparks that have inflamed
> their hearts. (*Inf.* 6.64–75)

The language of this response—suggestive but riddling—is
typical of prophecy. It must be decoded. Ciacco begins by alluding to the ousting of one party by another. In Dante's time,
there were two factions of the Guelf party: the Blacks, who supported the papacy, and the Whites, who supported the emperor.
Ciacco's answer to the first question ("what the citizens of the
divided city will come to"?) alludes to specific historical events
involving these two parties. Here he refers to a brawl that took
place on May 1, 1300, in Florence's Piazza di Santa Trinità
between rival members of the Black and White parties. Ciacco
predicts that "they will come to blood," and, in fact, during this

skirmish, a member of a powerful White family had his nose cut off. As a result, numerous prominent Blacks were exiled. In less than three years, however, the political situation changed, and the Blacks prevailed. Ciacco alludes directly to this change in the phrase "within three years."

The Blacks will regain power with the aid of "the power of one who presently is temporizing." Dante's earliest commentators usually see this as a reference to Pope Boniface VIII or his peacemaker, Charles of Valois, brother of the King of France, who is biding his time perhaps off the shores of Tuscany. The characterization of one party as the "rustic party" is a way of alluding to families from outside Florence, from rural areas, such as the present-day towns of Fiesole and Figline. The phrase "heavy burdens" might refer to the severe measures the Blacks imposed on the Whites: disqualification from holding public office and heavy taxes.

To Dante's second question, Ciacco answers "Two men are just." It is not clear whether he is referring to two just men or is indicating, by the number two, how few just men there are in Florence. This is the conventional language of prophecy—sonorous but opaque, hinting at knowledge just beyond our reach. Dante's third question concerns the reason why "such discord has assailed" Florence. The sins of pride, envy, and avarice are the source of all the civic discord. Ciacco's answer presents Florence as a sin-ridden city, torn asunder by deadly divisions. We have the impression that the Florentines had lost all sense of justice. The "divided city" is the result of a larger collapse of political institutions and social mores.

The exchange over local Florentine politics clarifies one of the strategies of dating the pilgrim's journey through the afterlife in 1300. Some of the "prophesies" simply repeat the past—events that had already taken place and whose consequences Dante, as he writes the poem, already knows. This time-scheme has the immediate effect of lending authority to the individual making the prophecy, whose other arguably prophetic utterances then gain a kind of weight. By mingling prophecy of two kinds—known (because it has already happened) and unknown—Dante lends these events a much broader and meaningful perspective. The ongoing analyses of Florentine and Italian politics are crucial to the social and religious reform that Dante seeks to effect. Through these encounters we come to understand the source, causes, and effects of internal division within the city. The sixth canto of each of the three parts of the *Divine Comedy* addresses "political" concerns: Through them, in succession, Dante advances from an account of the causes of division in Florence in the *Inferno* to those sundering Italy in *Purgatory* and finally the entire empire in *Paradise*. The perspective expands from the local to the universal as we are ultimately afforded a providential view of history.

The presentation here sets a pattern for many encounters in Dante's poem. We have a presumably historical character who, although his history is obscure to us, is profoundly engaged in historical events and the forces behind them. By presenting Ciacco in this way, Dante's poem opens a gap that is at once a mystery, if one seeks to fill it by searching the historical record, and an opportunity, if one is writing in the tradition of Dante's epic. What Dante leaves out in his presentation, writers following in his wake are happy to fill in.

## CONFRONTING WRATH: FILIPPO ARGENTI

Dante's encounter with another Florentine, the wrathful Filippo Argenti, presents readers with questions and puzzles of a different nature. Although we know more about the historical Filippo Argenti than about Ciacco, we do not know enough to understand why Dante treats him so harshly. Filippo bursts on the scene as Phlegyas, the boatman of the Styx, ferries Dante and Virgil across the filthy swamp. The wrathful, those who were unable to control their anger, are immersed in the bog. The counterpenalty is clear: Just as rage clouded their judgment in life, so does the thick mud envelop and blind them in Hell.

As they cross the river, Filippo tries to topple the boat, setting the scene for a violent face-off between him and Dante:

> While we were running through the dead channel, there rose before me one covered with mud, and said, "Who are you that come before your time?"
>
> And I to him, "If I come, I do not remain. But you, who are you that have become so foul?"
>
> He answered, "You see that I am one who weeps."
>
> And I to him, "In weeping and in sorrow do you remain, accursed spirit, for I know you, even if you are all filthy."
>
> Then he stretched both his hands to the boat, whereat the wary master thrust him off, saying, "Away there with the other dogs!" (*Inf.* 8.31–42)

This explosive scene is like no other we've seen so far. Despite the fact that Filippo Argenti does not want to reveal his name, Dante will make a point of trumpeting it—memorializing Filippo's damnation for the living. The way in which the two insult one another also merits notice: Each repeats the other's words (i.e., "I am one who weeps," "in weeping and in sorrow do you remain") to mock and infuriate one another.

Virgil's behavior surprises us as well: He approves of Dante's hostile reaction to Filippo. This is the only episode in the poem in which the guide approves so resoundingly the pilgrim's cruel treatment of another soul. When Dante expresses a keen eagerness to see the other angry souls attack Filippo, Virgil assures him that this wish will soon be gratified. Revenge does not get sweeter than this.

A little after this I saw such rending of him by the muddy folk
that I still praise and thank God for it. All cried, "At Filippo
Argenti!"—and the irascible Florentine spirit turned on himself with his teeth. (*Inf.* 8.58–63)

The change in language here—to torture and dismemberment—
comes as a shock: What seemed a nasty punishment now becomes horrible. Many modern readers find Dante's glee at the
sight of Filippo's dismemberment puzzling. Such vindictive sentiments contrast dramatically with the compassion the pilgrim
shows for souls encountered in earlier cantos: He fainted upon
hearing Francesca's poignant story, wept over Ciacco's fate, and
confessed himself to be "heart-wrung" at the sight of the punishment of the avaricious and the prodigal, who roll enormous
boulders endlessly in a circle.

The pilgrim's anger and Virgil's endorsement of it raise a
number of questions. The poem provides little evidence of why
this cruelty is justified. What little we know about this person
clarifies this scene in part, but not entirely. Filippo Argenti was
a Florentine nobleman, a member of the Adimari family, and a
Black Guelf. The Adimari were a wealthy family well known
for their persecution of others: Filippo himself was a notorious
hotheaded bully. He was not just a bully, but one who flaunted
his wealth—Filippo Argenti was said to have made silver horseshoes for his horses—hence the nickname Argenti, which recalls "*argento,*" the word for "silver."

Perhaps there was a personal side to Dante's hostile treatment of this damned soul, in that Filippo's brother usurped
the poet's goods after his exile. According to other accounts,
the Adimari violently opposed Dante's return from exile.
Other early readers say that Filippo once slapped Dante's face
during a quarrel. Again, in the absence of a clear historical
record, we have a colorful tradition of embellishment, specu-
lation, and storytelling. (Boccaccio's story about Ciacco also

includes Filippo Argenti.) This episode reminds us of how Dante's choices in writing create certain gaps in the poem. If early readers and subsequent investigations have been unable to pinpoint the identities of some of Dante's characters, later writers can create their own stories about these people or adapt the punishments.

Francesca, Ciacco, and Filippo Argenti are but three of the many encounters Dante has with Italians in the *Comedy*. He meets more contemporaries in Hell than in the other two realms of the afterlife. Many of these exchanges—notably those with Farinata degli Uberti, the captain of the Ghibelline party (*Inf.* 10); Brunetto Latini, a notary, philosopher, and teacher of rhetoric (*Inf.* 15); and Ugolino, a powerful Ghibelline nobleman (*Inf.* 33)—are among the most famous episodes of the *Inferno*.

These cantos show the tension in the poem that Dante's choice of local emphasis generates. Dante refers to figures like Homer and Aristotle in Limbo (*Inf.* 4) with spare references to who they were and what they did. He expects the reader to supply what is necessary for understanding the poem. (For modern readers, that means a quick glance at the explanatory notes to the particular edition of the *Inferno* they are reading.) What is notable here is that Dante seems to expect the same level of preparation on the part of the reader for the mention of Francesca, Ciacco, and Filippo Argenti. It is as if the poet expects readers to automatically recognize something prominent and memorable about Ciacco and Filippo. But, as mentioned, time has made obscure the lives of many of Dante's historical characters. No historian saw fit to record the circumstances of their lives in the detail necessary to understand Dante's references fully. Dante treats his contemporaries as if they would be as well known as classical, biblical, and mythological figures. This structural feature of Dante's poem provides the gaps and spaces that subsequent writers can exploit.

## LOCAL AND MYTHIC IN LOWER HELL

If we look at sections of the *Inferno* that contain both classical and historical people, we see that Dante the pilgrim chooses to focus on contemporary Italians again and again. Canto 18 demonstrates this point dramatically. Here we meet two groups of sinners—the panderers and seducers, who are grouped together and whipped by a devil, and the flatterers, who are immersed in excrement. A number of details highlight Dante's interest in the local. He describes the encounter with his contemporary Venedico Caccianemico before turning his attention to Jason, the fabled adventurer. Despite Jason's long list of exploits, Dante devotes more lines to the meeting with Venedico. The pilgrim recognizes Venedico immediately, although the man does not wish to be recognized. Venedico Caccianemico was a Guelf leader of Bologna and the political head of several cities. Venedico confesses his sordid crime without hesitation, compelled, as he puts it, by Dante's "plain speech": "I was he who brought Ghisolabella to do the will of the Marquis, however the vile story may be reported" (*Inf.* 18.55–57). As his succinct identification reveals, Venedico is damned for currying favor with the Marquis of Este by pimping his sister, Ghisolabella, in exchange for money and political favors.

Not only does the pilgrim show little interest in Jason's fabled adventure, he resolutely pursues details more historical than mythical. Even the language of the encounter with Venedico smacks of local concerns. Venedico informs Dante that he is not the only Bolognese pimp there.

> And I am not the only Bolognese who laments here; nay, this place is so full of them, that so many tongues are not now taught, between Savena and Reno, to say *sipa;* and if of this you wish assurance or testimony, recall to mind our avaricious nature. (*Inf.* 18.58–63)

Most translators do not translate the word *"sipa,"* medieval
Bolognese dialect for "yes." Dante exploits a regional expres-
sion to heighten the particularly Bolognese aspect of this sin:
This region of Hell teems with panderers from Bologna.

Dante's emphasis here could not be more stark. Virgil
points out Jason's kingly demeanor, how impervious he seems
to his punishment, and his ardent pursuit of the Golden Fleece.
Dante's guide recounts Jason's amorous exploits: his seduction
of Hypsipyle "with tokens and fair words," his abandonment
of her "pregnant and forlorn," his treacherous affair with Me-
dea, and his eventual desertion of her to marry Creusa. Dante,
pointedly silent, merely observes him. Despite Jason's fame and
notoriety, Dante prefers to engage Venedico.

Another classical/historical pairing also highlights the
prominence Dante gives contemporary figures. After seeing the
panderers and seducers, Dante comes upon the flatterers. Dante
classifies flattery as a form of fraud, because it distorts social
interactions by exaggeration and outright misrepresentation.
Court life, with its arcane privileges and byzantine patron–client relations, might well be said to encourage flattery by its
very structure. The contrapasso here—flatters are immersed in
excrement—seems particularly obvious to modern readers, for
whom terms like "bullshit" and "crap" are commonplace, even
habitual. Dante adds another level of consideration, however.
He is always sensitive to the abuse of language, clearly because
he considers it more damaging to the community than other
sins—even sins such as murder.

Among the flatterers, Dante meets the contemporary Alessio Interminei, a member of a powerful noble Lucchese family,
and Thaïs, a Greek courtesan in a play by Terence. Dante introduces us first to Alessio:

> Hither we came, and thence I saw down in the ditch a people
> plunged in filth that seemed to have come from human privies.

> And while I was searching down there with my eyes, I beheld one whose head was so befouled with ordure that it did not appear whether he was layman or cleric. He bawled to me, "Why are you so greedy to look more at me than at the other filthy ones?" And I to him, "Because, if I rightly recall, I have seen you with your hair dry, and you are Alessio Interminei of Lucca; therefore do I eye you more than all the rest." (*Inf.* 18.112–123)

Few descriptions of the damned are more graphically disgusting than Dante's portrait of Alessio. Again, part of the horror of sin is the transformed appearance of the sinner, who often becomes anonymous. Alessio's head is "befouled with ordure," making it impossible to see if his head is tonsured or not. (Clergymen were tonsured, making them recognizable; Interminei, covered in shit, cannot be categorized.) As in the case of Filippo Argenti earlier, Dante takes evident pleasure in naming this notoriously unctuous flatterer. He also seems to relish the opportunity to insult him, even to mock him. Dante sarcastically declares he's seen Alessio when his head was "dry," that is, when he was alive and not covered in excrement.

By contrast, Thaïs is reduced to pure spectacle, albeit of a disgusting kind: She scratches herself with her "filthy [literally shit-filled] nails." Dante does not engage her. His interest lies in historical figures, and this interest is insistent. Dante makes a bold choice in his representation of Hell, and he wants his reader to be aware of this decision.

Classical figures dominate elsewhere in Hell. No reader of the *Inferno* can forget Ulysses, whose speech in canto 26 is one of the high points of literature. But more typically classical figures are simply presented as spectacle. In *Inferno* 14, Dante meets Capaneus, a mythical warrior-king who besieged Thebes along with six other kings. Significantly, Dante does not speak to Capaneus: The pilgrim observes him as Virgil points out the blasphemer's intransigence. Dante's encounters with other classical figures in lower Hell are similarly uneventful. When Dante meets the sorceress Manto in *Inferno* 20 and Curio, a Roman tribune, in *Inferno* 28, Virgil instructs and Dante listens. He does not engage these souls directly. Often the reference simply registers the presence of these figures, as if Dante were a tourist ticking off various sights on a list. Again and again Dante returns our attention to contemporary Italians, as if he feels that stories of familiar men and women will resonate more deeply with his readers. Over time, characters such as Francesca have become famous in their own right. In exploiting the local, Dante not only introduces a new category of people to the epic tradition, but he also opens up a new arena for creative exploitation by later writers who personalize the afterlife in imaginative and provocative ways. This decision constitutes one of the most original features of Dante's masterpiece.

# A Divided World

## Politics, War, and Exile

One might think that during his journey, a trip concerned with personal salvation, Dante would pay little attention to politics and partisan strife. In the world of the *Divine Comedy*, however, these subjects loom large. Italy was not a unified country in the thirteenth century. Charlemagne's conquest of northern Italy in 774 and his subsequent coronation in 800 had established him as Holy Roman Emperor. But this order could not hold. After a nearly 50-year struggle, by 1122, the pope as well as various city-states had won independence from imperial control. These regional divisions contributed to a continuous state of strife and warfare.

Dante blamed the many wars and skirmishes on the absence of an emperor in Rome and a series of power-hungry popes. The fact that the German Hohenstaufen emperor (to whom mantle of Holy Roman Emperor had passed) preferred to stay in Germany left the papacy ample opportunity to expand its influence and territorial holdings. Dante took a very dim view of this activity and of the inaction of the Holy Roman Emperor. Having seen firsthand the results of factionalism, he devotes considerable attention to an analysis of its causes and effects in the *Inferno*. As one might expect, in the *Inferno* Dante doesn't discuss politics in theoretical terms but immerses himself in the details and particulars of political factions. The vast majority of political allusions in the poem deal with the political situation of Dante's Italy and his own Florence. Once again we see how Dante's bias toward the local and nearby affects the poem's ultimate shape.

## GUELFS AND GHIBELLINES

The Guelfs and Ghibellines were the two main parties of medieval Italy. The Guelfs—whose name derived from Welf, an illustrious German dynasty—allied themselves with the papacy, effectively becoming a party of the church. The Ghibellines—a name derived from Weiblingen, a German castle—supported the German emperors. Intent on keeping the German emperor out of Italy, the Guelfs allied themselves with the French monarchy. In central Italy, various towns allied themselves with one of the two parties. For example, Bologna, Florence, Montepulciano, Orvieto, Lucca, and Genoa supported the Guelfs. Pistoia, Arezzo, Pisa, and Siena aligned themselves with the Ghibellines. Between 1260 and 1315, there were six wars between the Guelfs and Ghibellines, not to mention many smaller outbreaks of violence. After the Battle of Benevento (1266), in which the Guelfs, led by the French Charles I of Anjou, defeated the Ghibellines, led by Manfred, the illegitimate son of the German Emperor Frederick II, the Ghibellines' power was greatly diminished. Defeat did not bring peace, however. The Guelf party split into two factions, known as the Black Guelfs and White Guelfs (or simply Blacks and Whites). The Blacks allied themselves with the Guelfs; the Whites, with the former Ghibellines. The terms "Blacks" and "Whites" were taken from the names of two rival factions in Pistoia, a Tuscan town.

Dante turns to the history of party strife and its repercussions again and again in the *Inferno*. Through his meetings with numerous contemporary figures, he explores the causes underlying the divisions that sunder not just Florence but Italy and the empire more generally. This preoccupation also has a personal dimension: Dante's exile from Florence resulted directly from divisions between the Blacks and the Whites. Throughout the poem Dante deftly weaves references to his exile into his exchanges with various souls and by so doing inextricably intertwines the personal and the political.

## THE BLACKEST SOULS IN HELL

Dante carefully lays the basis for his examination of politics in *Inferno* 6. As we saw in chapter 2, Dante quickly turns the conversation to politics when he meets Ciacco. The glutton's prophecy invites deeper consideration of the historical events familiar to early readers of the poem. Ultimately, through this heightened scrutiny of causes and consequences, Dante places historical events into a larger scheme—at once human and providential. Prophecy suggests that history has coherence and meaning, that it is a story, not simply a chronicle of what happens.

*Inferno* 6, along with other cantos that address local political issues, is crucial to the social and religious reform that Dante seeks. Generally, Dante effects these changes in one of two ways: He directly criticizes the deplorable conditions of the present or offers an indirect critique by praising the virtues and customs of the past. In the meeting with Ciacco, he criticizes Florence's current civic woes. After Ciacco answers Dante's three questions, Dante asks Ciacco about the fate of five men:

"Farinata and Tegghiaio, who were so worthy, Jacopo Rusticucci, Arrigo, and Mosca, and the others who set their minds
on doing good, tell me where they are and give me to know
them, for great desire urges me to learn whether Heaven
soothes or Hell envenoms them."

And he, "They are among the blackest souls, and different faults weigh them down toward the bottom; if you
descend that far, there you can see them." (*Inf.* 6.79–87)

Why these five men in particular? one might ask. The identity of Arrigo, a character Dante does not mention again, is unknown, and one of the enduring mysteries of the poem, but the
other four names refer to prominent political figures from an
earlier generation. Dante singles out four figures closely aligned
with key political events rather than other sinners. He names no
classical figures in this group, and he does not have a face-to-
face encounter with someone from ancient times until he meets
the blasphemer Capaneus in *Inferno* 14. Not only are the five
men Italians; three of them—Farinata, Tegghiaio, and Jacopo
Rusticucci—were involved in one of the period's bloodiest battles, the Battle of Montaperti (1260). Mosca is associated with
the event that led to the Guelf-Ghibelline split. This history
forms a rich context for Dante's innocent question about their
salvation or damnation. Ciacco responds unequivocally. All
damned, they are among the "blackest" souls in Hell: We find
Farinata among the heretics, Tegghiaio and Jacopo Rusticucci
with the sodomites, and Mosca among the sowers of discord.

## FARINATA AND THE CARNAGE OF MONTAPERTI

Dante the pilgrim has long been anticipating his meeting with
Farinata, and Dante the poet takes care that we share this an-
ticipation. Of all the discussions of politics in the *Inferno,* this
is the most momentous. Dante's excitement is evident from the

beginning of the canto, where he tells Virgil of his desire to see the souls within the burning tombs. Since he would have known that Farinata had been condemned while alive as a heretic, Dante likely had some presentiment that this soul would be among the heretics in Hell.

The heretics are the first souls that the two wayfarers see upon passing through the gates to Dis, the city of Lower Hell. Dante compares the landscape of the sixth circle to an immense necropolis, a comparison that exemplifies his frequent references to real places in order to help readers visualize the varied landscapes he discusses. This huge graveyard resembles the stone tombs at Arles in southern France and at Pola, another Roman necropolis on the Istrian peninsula. (See figure 3.)

The clarity of his vision underscores Dante's considerable poetic craft. He builds on living traditions in constructing this circle. First of all, Dante distinguishes the heretics from the souls in Limbo. Heretics willfully deny the existence of God or defy church doctrine. (The virtuous heathens in Limbo—as

Fig. 3.   Tombs at Alyscamps, Arles, Photo by Deborah Parker.

well as the souls of unbaptized children—were simply unaware
of God.) Second, Dante mentions only one of the heretical sects
housed in the circle—the Epicureans, who denied the immor-
tality of the soul. Having simplified heresy to willful denial of
any afterlife, Dante proceeds to link the infernal and everlasting punishment of the heretics with their historical punishment
on Earth. The fire he sees emerging from the tombs recalls the
medieval sentence for heresy, burning at the stake. The irony is
sharp. Those who denied an eternal life are eternally burned,
and their afterlife becomes a kind of living death.

Dante addresses two senses at once. The visual element—
sinners roasting in tombs—is perhaps strongest, but the sinners' lamentations engage the sense of hearing powerfully as
well. As the pilgrim approaches the tombs, he hears a voice
issuing from one. Farinata, recognizing that Dante is Florentine from his accent, seeks news of his native city. This initial
polite exchange is short-lived. Once the conversation turns to
politics, we see that Farinata's intense attachment to political
affairs precludes thoughts of anything else for the Ghibelline
leader. How Dante responds, however, comes as something of
a surprise. He is so startled by this voice that he is stunned into
silence. Virgil has to prompt him; he urges Dante to snap out
of it and face Farinata.

> "Turn round! what are you doing? See there Farinata who
> has risen erect: from the waist upwards you will see him all."
>
> Already I had fixed my eyes on his, and he rose upright
> with chest and brow thrown back as if he had great scorn of
> Hell; and the bold and ready hands of my leader pushed me
> between the tombs to him, and he said, "Let your words be
> fitting." (*Inf.* 10.31–39)

One of the most imposing souls in Hell, Farinata rises from
within the tomb, visible from the waist up. Cavalcanti, the
other figure encountered here, rises only enough to make his

chin visible. Standing formidably before Dante, Farinata appears "as if he had great scorn of Hell" (*Inf.* 10.36). Virgil, almost acting the part of a pushy stage mother, thrusts Dante out among the sepulchers.

Farinata, the Ghibelline captain, immediately takes control of the conversation and interrogates Dante, asking who his ancestors were. This question shows Farinata's obsession with politics, more specifically with party allegiances. From this point on, Farinata's attitude toward Dante hinges entirely on this question—whether the two belong to the same party or not. For the military man, clarity is necessary: Were you for me or against me? Dante answers the question fully, informing Farinata that his family were Guelfs. (Although Dante has sympathies for the Ghibelline cause, in this canto he assumes the role of a Guelf.) Farinata reacts to the poet's answer by raising his eyebrows, indicating his disdain at finding himself before a member of the minor nobility and a Guelf.

Farinata's subtle response exemplifies Dante's brilliant use of gesture. In the brief encounters that take place between the pilgrim and the souls of the afterlife, raised eyebrows, an upturned face, or a finger placed over one's mouth all serve to enhance the presentation of the souls. Part of Dante's genius as a poet lies in his extraordinary ability to reduce a complex situation to gestures that are still understandable today.

Once the topic turns to local politics, all pleasantries disappear. The meeting quickly degenerates into a terse exchange of insults along party lines.

> And I, who was eager to obey, concealed nothing, but made all plain to him; whereupon he raised his brows a little; then he said, "They were fiercely adverse to me and to my forebears and to my party, so that twice over I scattered them."
>
> "If they were driven forth, they returned from every quarter, both times," I answered him, "but yours have not learned that art well." (*Inf.* 10.43–51)

Upon learning that Dante's family was Guelf, Farinata responds to Dante as an enemy. He does not mince words, declaring that the actions of Dante's ancestors warranted a violent response. Farinata boasts of having scattered his enemies twice. Here he alludes to an event in 1248 in which he led a Ghibelline force that drove the Guelfs out of Florence; then to the Battle of Montaperti, in which exiled Sienese and Florentine Ghibellines defeated the Florentine Guelfs at Montaperti, a plain outside Siena.

Despite his initial reticence, Dante answers boldly. Indeed, he goes Farinata one better, wounding the Ghibelline captain by pointing out that if the Guelfs ("his party") were "driven forth," at least they returned to Florence each time, first in 1266 after the Battle of Benevento, when Charles I of Anjou defeated King Manfred and the Ghibellines, then in 1268 at the Battle of Tagliacozzo, when Charles I defeated Frederick II's grandson, Conradin. In his final taunt, Dante tells Farinata that the Ghibellines never learned the very difficult art of returning from exile.

The exchange between the two Florentines has become testy. In adopting the rhetoric of his Guelf ancestors, Dante effectively embraces and perpetrates a schism that had divided Florence even before he was born. The argument typifies political debates of the times. If Farinata's remarks show that he is still clearly bound up with the political situation in Florence—even while burning eternally—Dante's response indicates that he cannot resist being drawn in even as he makes a spiritual pilgrimage. Their tense exchange ends with the pilgrim's stinging retort. With this zinger, Farinata is momentarily silenced while Dante speaks with another soul, Cavalcante de' Cavalcanti, who seeks information of a more personal nature. He wishes to know why his son Guido, as gifted intellectually as Dante, does not accompany the poet on this journey.

Then the conversation between Dante and Farinata resumes at exactly the point where it had broken off. Farinata matches

Dante's rejoinder that the Ghibellines never returned to Florence by predicting Dante's own exile: "But the face of the Lady who rules here will not be kindled fifty times before you shall know how much that art weighs" (*Inf.* 10.79–81). This is the second prediction of Dante's exile in the poem. Ciacco had alluded to it earlier when he predicted that within "three years," the "rustic party" (the Whites) would fall (*Inf.* 6.67).

Like the language of all other prophecies in the poem, this one is couched in mysterious terms that the reader must unravel. The "face of the Lady" refers to the mythical figure of Persephone, who was identified with the moon. Hence within 50 months—more precisely, in June 1304—Dante, who during the initial phase of his exile had thrown in his lot with other exiled White Guelfs, would learn that his hopes for returning to Florence were in vain. Farinata's prediction shows how Dante's destiny will soon come to resemble his own. That the Ghibellines never learned the "difficult art" of returning from exile torments Farinata more than the punishments of Hell. The personal and the political could not be more closely connected.

In a wider sense, Farinata's prophecy undercuts the entire debate with Dante. One can, as Farinata seeks to do, insist on the simplicity of every situation. One can identify one's enemies in a series of direct questions and act accordingly. But exile is the end for both sides to this exchange, and this unexpected shared experience suggests that the differences, however heated and however consuming, are less absolute than each side thinks.

The concerns Farinata expresses next reveal a shift from the exclusively political to what might be termed the familial. Farinata's preoccupations begin to resemble those of Cavalcanti, who was worried about the fate of his son. This is evident in Farinata's next question to Dante: "why is that people so fierce against my kindred in all its laws?" (*Inf.* 10.83–84). Farinata even prefaces his question with kind regard for Dante—"And so you may return some time to the sweet world." For someone as civically engaged as Farinata, the world was everything. In 1283, Farinata was excommunicated; his remains were exhumed and scattered. All the goods of his heirs were confiscated. The focus in the exchange has shifted to Florence's responsibilities toward its future generations: We see two parallel stories in Dante's exile and the fate of Farinata's descendants. Florentine officials banished Dante's children along with the poet. Thus while Dante and Farinata belong to two different political parties, their descendants suffer a similar injustice—exile caused by party strife.

Dante answers that the Florentines cannot forget the Battle of Montaperti. Roughly 10,000 Florentines died during the fighting, which pitted 30,000 Florentines against 20,000 Sienese and imperial troops. So many died that the blood of the fallen stained the river Arbia red. The memory of this carnage lies behind the enmity of Florentines toward Farinata.

The mention of Montaperti summons painful memories, as we see in another expressive gesture. Farinata shakes his head and he replies that he did not act alone in that battle. Where he did stand alone, however, was at the parliament at Empoli that took place after the battle. While the other Ghibellines wanted to raze Florence, Farinata defended the city against complete destruction. At this point, we have come full circle. Farinata has defined himself once again and above all as a Florentine, not only a Ghibelline—just as he had done in his first words to Dante.

## BRUNETTO AND THE MIXED
## ORIGINS OF FLORENCE

Dante's meeting with Farinata highlights past political division—the bitterness of the tensions between the two parties and the durability of these enmities. In his meeting with Brunetto Latini, Dante continues and expands his exploration of

the causes of Florence's long-standing internal divisions. Brunetto Latini (1220–1294) was a rhetorician, moralist, poet, and
public servant. Forty-five years old when Dante was born, Brunetto represents a previous generation of political fellow travelers. While on a diplomatic mission in Spain, Brunetto learned
that his party, the Guelfs, had been defeated at Montaperti. He
took refuge in France and returned to Florence in 1266 after the
Ghibellines were defeated that year at the Battle of Benevento.
While in France, Brunetto wrote two encyclopedias—the *Tesoro*
(Treasure) and the *Tesoretto* (Little Treasure), two medieval
compendiums of history, natural science, ethics, and rhetoric.
After the Guelf triumph at Benevento, Brunetto lived in Florence until his death in 1294. Strong connections exist between
Dante and this sinner. Not only is he a member of Dante's party,
the Guelfs, but, as Brunetto's last words in the canto—"Let my
*Treasure,* in which I live, be commended to you"—make clear,
the two also share the vocation of writer. Finally, Brunetto was
something of a mentor to Dante.

Brunetto, damned for sodomy (the juridical term for homosexuality in the Middle Ages), appears in one of the most
complicated of Dante's nine circles of Hell. The seventh circle,
which punishes the violent, consists of three rings—one containing those who are violent against others, the second holding the suicides or those who are violent against the self, and
an inner ring confining those violent against God. This inner
ring punishes blasphemy, sodomy, and usury. The damned in
this ring inhabit a barren desert, where a rain of fire, which
descends in flakes, desiccates the landscape and scorches them,
making their baked and blistered features nearly unrecogniz-
able. The fire from above ignites the sand beneath their feet,
doubling their torment.

The meeting between Dante and Brunetto is the most
personal of all the encounters in Hell. It is not possible to

reconstruct the exact nature of the relationship between the elderly Brunetto and the young Dante, who was 29 when Brunetto died. We should probably take Dante at his words: Most likely he had learned something about philosophy, civic leadership, and rhetoric and versification from reading Brunetto's works. All that can be said with certainty is that Dante knew the man personally and learned from him and that this contact underlies one of the most ambiguous and elusive episodes in the entire poem, in which Dante both immortalizes and condemns Brunetto. The presentation, as with the presentation of Paolo, Francesca, and Farinata, is unusually complex. Dante considers Brunetto unrepentant—an inveterate sodomite—and he condemns him according to the laws implicit in the plan of Hell. But he remembers, with real affection and esteem, the nobility of his former teacher's character. The last view of Brunetto is one of affirmation. He runs like a sprinter, and "he who wins, not he who loses" (*Inf.* 15.124).

After a recognition scene, the two discuss a wide range of topics, among them the eternal movement of the souls (lines 34–42), Dante's journey home with the guidance of Virgil (lines 46–54), Dante's potential glorious destiny (lines 55–60), as well as the corruption of the Fiesolan Florentines and their future persecution of Dante by exile (lines 61–78). The encounter culminates in Dante's elegant recollection of the core of Brunetto's teaching. Dante remembers his mentor, even as he damns him, as the one who taught him "how man makes himself eternal"— that is, through the pursuit of worldly fame. By the end of their exchange, the pilgrim displays a newfound stalwartness: He stands prepared for whatever Fortune has in store for him (lines 88–99). Henceforth, Dante will no longer be surprised or daunted by allusions to his exile.

Brunetto's comments on the origins of Florence provide further insight into the fractious nature of the Florentines: The schism that plagues the city has deep roots. Before turning to the subject of politics, Brunetto informs the pilgrim that he had long foreseen a glorious destiny for Dante and regrets not having had the opportunity to impart more of his teachings to him. The endless party skirmishes that plagued Florence, not to mention Brunetto's death, prevented him from passing on any further civic and political lessons. However, Brunetto makes the most of the time he now has. Beginning in line 61, he explains the causes underlying the warring nature of Florentines.

> But that thankless, malignant people, who of old came down from Fiesole, and still smack of the mountain and the rock, will make themselves an enemy to you because of your good deeds; and there is cause: for among the bitter sorb-trees it is not fitting that the sweet fig should come to fruit. Old report in the world calls them blind; it is a people avaricious, envious and proud: look that you cleanse yourself of their customs. Your fortune holds for you such honor that the one party and the other shall be ravenous against you, but the grass shall be far from the goat. Let the Fiesolan beasts make fodder of themselves, and not touch the plant (if any spring yet upon their dungheap) in which survives the holy seed of those Romans who remained there when it became of the nest of so much wickedness." (*Inf.* 15.61–78)

All of Dante's bitterness over his exile and his disgust with the rancor and corruption of Florentine politics emerges in Brunetto's scornful invective. This condemnation of the Florentines as "blind . . . avaricious, envious and proud" echoes Ciacco's characterization of them as proud, envious, and avaricious in *Inferno* 6. More significantly, Brunetto blames the divisiveness of Florentines on the city's mixed origins: Florentines descend from the "thankless," hard, flinty inhabitants of Fiesole, a town near Florence, as well as from the noble Romans. The mixed origins of Florence refer to a legend concerning the city's founding. In classical times, Romans pursued Catiline, a politician who sought to overthrow the republic, to the environs of present-day Fiesole. After a pitched battle, they decimated his army and killed him. Liking the spot, the Romans decided to settle in the area. As the rustic Fiesolans already occupied this area, the two peoples mixed. Descended from this incongruous mix, Florentines are ever divided among themselves.

After this searing characterization of his fellow citizens, Brunetto turns to their malice toward Dante in line 64: "because of your good deeds" (presumably Dante's good civic deeds), they will become his enemies. Thus Dante, the "sweet fig" of line 66, must steer clear of his bellicose fellow citizens because no fruit can thrive in so hostile a climate. Both parties (the Blacks and the Whites) will be hungry for Dante and desire to have him in their midst. But, Brunetto cautions, the "grass" (Dante) must evade the "goat" (his bestial fellow exiles). Viewed in historical terms, the other exiled Whites will want to vent their frustration on Dante because of disagreements within the party over how best to return to Florence after their banishment.

Brunetto's prophecy becomes at once more loose and more powerful as he pursues it. In counseling Dante to keep the grass "far from the goat," he builds on the allusion to the poet as a sweet fig earlier. The savage Fiesolans should be left to forage among themselves. "Plant" (line 74), however, refers not only to the fig. It also evokes the "holy seed" of the Florentines of Roman stock. Amid the "dungheap" of a malicious, arrogant, and ungrateful people, the "sweet fig" might yet take root. Even here Dante adds a complexity to his vision. Dung might choke the "holy seed of those Romans" who still survive in the city, but that same dung might fertilize the field.

From beyond the grave, Brunetto seeks to prepare Dante for the adversity he will soon encounter upon his exile. Hearing these warnings about his future, Dante tells Brunetto that he will heed the lesson imparted, holding it "with a text to be glossed by a lady." Dante will preserve the earlier references to his exile he has heard in the journey so far until his meeting Beatrice further clarifies their meaning. (Ultimately it is Cacciaguida, the poet's great-great-grandfather, who enlightens him.)

> That which you tell me of my course I write, and keep with a text to be glossed by a lady who will know how, if I reach her. This much I would have you know: so conscience chide me not, I am prepared for Fortune as she wills. Such earnest is not strange to my ears; therefore let Fortune whirl her wheel as pleases her, and the yokel his mattock. (*Inf.* 15.88–96)

In lines 91 to 96, Dante declares himself braced for the vagaries of Fortune, whose mythical action of turning a wheel he likens to the familiar action of a peasant wielding a hoe. Dante has come a long way since his meeting with Ciacco, when he received the first intimations of his exile. Farinata's prediction made it explicit, and Brunetto's prophecy clarifies it. While no less invested in local politics, Dante accepts his fate stoically. Ultimately, the poet will analyze the causes of evil in the world in more philosophical terms in Purgatory and Paradise. While still in Hell, however, Dante grounds his analysis of Florence's political ills firmly in reality. We are still very much in the realm of the practical.

## THE SEEDS OF CORRUPTION

Dante continues his analysis of the problems plaguing his city in the next canto, where he meets more Florentines. We have been anticipating a meeting with two of these individuals since *Inferno* 6, where Dante had inquired about the fate of Tegghiaio and Jacopo Rusticucci, among others. The central action of the canto begins when three souls approach Dante in search

of some authoritative word about the state of Florence. The
three form a kind of chorus, moving together with an elaborate
wheeling motion, keeping their faces to Dante as they rotate
amid the flakes of fire. One soul, Jacopo Rusticucci, introduces
himself and his companions:

> grandson of the good Gualdrada, his name was Guido Guer-
> ra, and in his lifetime he did much with counsel and with
> sword. This other, who treads the sand behind me, is Teg-
> ghiaio Aldobrandi, whose voice should have been prized up
> in the world; and I who am placed with them in torment was
> Jacopo Rusticucci, and truly my fierce wife more than aught
> else has wrought me ill. (*Inf.* 16.37–45)

As in the encounter with Farinata, genealogy and political
affiliation are prominent. Jacopo Rusticucci introduces Guido
Guerra as the grandson of the "good Gualdrada"—Gualdrada
dei Ravagnani—renowned for her virtue and beauty. The chief
leader of the Tuscan Guelf party, Guido Guerra (1220–1272)
fought at the head of the Florentine troops at the Battle of
Montaperti. Although he tried to dissuade the Florentine
Guelfs from engaging Farinata and the Sienese Ghibellines, his
advice was unheeded. Later he helped restore the Guelfs to
power after the Battle of Benevento. The second man mentioned is Tegghiaio Aldobrandi, another chief of the Florentine
Guelfs at Montaperti. The counsel to which Jacopo Rusticucci
alludes in lines 42 and 43 concerns Tegghiaio's advice to the
Florentines not to fight the Sienese and Ghibelline troops at
Montaperti. Jacopo Rusticucci, whose name often appears
alongside Tegghiaio's in historical documents, assisted in the
negotiation of various peace treaties. In speaking of himself,
Jacopo implies in line 45 that his shrewish wife drove him to
homosexuality.[1]

*Inferno* 6, 10, 15, and 16 address the causes of Florence's divisions and its social consequences. Dante's treatment of this issue is by no means simple. By looking at the combined message offered by these cantos, we can obtain a better idea of the city's civic problems. In *Inferno* 6, Ciacco alluded to future civil strife caused by party divisions, noted the small number of just men in the city, and characterized Florentines as envious, proud, and avaricious. In the meeting with Farinata in *Inferno* 10, we saw how the battles of Montaperti and Benevento—bitter memories of carnage and exile—tore the community apart. In *Inferno* 15, Brunetto Latini blamed the civic strife on the mixed origins of the city. In this canto, the focus turns to the present. Dante begins by praising Jacopo Rusticucci, Tegghiaio, and Guido Guerra for their honorable civic deeds:

> I am of your city, and always have I rehearsed and heard with affection your deeds and honored names. I am leaving the gall, and I go for sweet fruits promised me by my truthful leader; but first I must go down to the center. (*Inf.* 16.58–63)

Their response is equally courteous. Jacopo Rusticucci then asks the pilgrim:

> "So may your soul long direct your limbs, and your fame shine after you," he then replied, "tell us if courtesy and valor abide in our city as once they did, or if they are quite gone from it . . ." (*Inf.* 16.64–9)

This question prompts a surprisingly direct outburst from the pilgrim:

> "The new people and the sudden gains have engendered pride and excess in you, O Florence, so that already you

weep for it!" This I cried with uplifted face; and the three,
who understood this to be my answer, looked at each other
as men look on hearing the truth. (*Inf.* 16.73–78)

What the three wish to know most is whether the values they
lived by still reign in Florence. For Dante, courtesy and valor
consist in virtue, exceptional manners, and liberality. Notwithstanding their private vices, Tegghaio, Jacopo Rusticucci, and
Guido Guerra all upheld noble civic virtues. It is for this reason that they are deserving of respect. These noble values have
long been replaced by more self-serving interests. Commercial
interests ("sudden gains") and immigration ("new people" to
the city) erode the social fabric of society, leading to moral
decay. Wealth breeds contemptible behavior—the selfishness,
self-aggrandizement, and pride exemplified by people like
Filippo Argenti, who frittered away his inheritance on vulgar
purchases, such as silver horseshoes. In line 73, Dante refers to
"newcomers," recalling the people mentioned by Ciacco in his
allusion to the "rustic party," families from the countryside.
Some of these "new people," Florence's newly rich, maintained
their wealth through usury. This newer generation lacks any
social or moral conscience. Vulgar upstarts with little sense of
civic responsibility have eclipsed the generation of Tegghiaio
and Guido Guerra.

In lines 61 to 63, Dante provides a compact statement of
the purpose of his journey. He leaves behind the "gall" so that
he might collect the "sweet fruits"—that is, Dante abandons a
worldly immersion in politics for the spiritual rewards of the
journey to Beatrice. But this succinct summation of purpose is
the product of a determinate process, recorded in cantos 6, 10,
15, and 16. Dante makes this emphatic in two ways. He uses
the term "gall" here to remind us of the agricultural imagery so
prominent in Brunetto's prophecy in the previous canto. And
perhaps more deliberately, Dante reorients the relationship of

the pilgrim to the damned over the course of these encounters. In the earlier meeting, Dante had asked Ciacco for news of Florence's future; here it is the damned who seek news about Florence's current situation. As the voyage progresses, so does Dante's education. It's natural that he now knows more than he did at the beginning of the journey. When Dante identifies commercial interests and quick wealth as the factors contributing to Florence's ruin, the three gaze upward, as people do when hearing the truth. The pilgrim has confirmed their worst suspicions.

## MOSCA AND POLITICAL FACTION

In *Inferno* 6, Dante had also asked Ciacco about Mosca's fate. In turning now to this figure, we move from sinners who are morally ambiguous to one who is thoroughly perfidious. Placed considerably lower in Hell than the others, Mosca is among the schismatics or sowers of discord in Malebolge, the eighth circle of Hell, which houses the fraudulent. Malebolge, which translates to "evil pits," is divided into ten rings. Among the sinners Dante encounters here are panderers and seducers, simonists (those who sell church offices and favors), barrators (corrupt public officials), diviners, hypocrites, thieves, false counselors, schismatics, and falsifiers.

The sowers of discord suffer one of Hell's most gruesome punishments. As they walk eternally around the ditch, a demon hacks them with a sword. Those who divided are now literally divided. Those who sundered the body politic now have their own bodies hewn, slashed, and lopped. *Inferno* 28 resembles nothing so much as a slaughterhouse run by a lunatic. The circle runs like clockwork as souls move around it. But the savage violence of the demon's sword disrupts this meticulous pattern. The souls encountered here include: Mohammed and Ali, founders of Islam who, according to Dante, created division within Christianity; Pier da Medicina, who sowed discord between two rival families; the Roman Curio, who urged Caesar to cross the Rubicon, an action that resulted in civil war; Mosca, who ignited hostilities between the Guelfs and Ghibellines; and Bertran de Born, a Provençal poet who incited Prince Henry to revolt against his father, Henry II of England. The wounds are savage as well as roughly emblematic of the types of division the schismatics created.

The demon slashes the sinners in imaginative ways: He splits Mohammed from chin to trunk, slices Ali from chin to hairline, clips and nicks Pier da Medicina in different places, hacks out Curio's tongue, lops off Mosca's hands, and decapitates Bertran. The contrapasso requires little explanation: Given how well the punishment fits the crime, it's no surprise that Dante chose this canto to introduce the term "contrapasso."

Mosca dei Lamberti possesses none of the redeeming qualities of Farinata, Brunetto, Tegghiaio, and Guido Guerra. An ardent Ghibelline, Mosca instigated the murder of Buondelmonte de' Buondelmonti, a nobleman who had jilted a young woman of the Amidei family. When the wronged family met with their allies to decide what to do about Buondelmonte's refusal to go through with the arranged marriage, Mosca responded tersely: "Capo ha cosa fatta," in other words, a "done deed finds its purpose" or "what's done is at an end." With this inflammatory quip—which, to modern audiences, might recall the succinct phrasing of the *Godfather* films—Mosca incited the bride's family to kill Buondelmonte. The Amidei confronted him while he was riding his horse near the Ponte Vecchio and brutally stabbed him to death.

In the eyes of Dante and many of his contemporaries, the murder of Buondelmonte was *the* foundational act that initiated the conflict between the Guelfs and Ghibellines. Hence Mosca becomes the poster child for political division. Dante's presentation of Mosca is memorably gruesome.

And one who had both hands lopped off, raising the stumps
through the murky air so that the blood befouled his face,
cried, "You will recall Mosca too who said, alas! 'A thing
done has an end!' which was seed of ill to the Tuscan people."
(*Inf.* 28.103–108)

Dante's punishment of Mosca plays on his famous quip. Mosca
may have thought that Buondelmonte's death would put an end
to the whole affair, but the murder ignited more violent strife.
Violence did not bring an end to this feud. Instead, the murder
of Buondelmonti began a cycle of exile and violence in Florence.
Viewed against Mosca's infamous statement, the repetitive nature of his punishment—the eternal tracing of the circle, regularly punctuated by dismemberment and mutilation—forms the
ultimate irony. Rarely does Dante's vision take the form of so
urgent a warning. Schism, whether religious, civil, or political,
is the poet's abiding horror, as the canto's slaughterhouse imagery makes apparent to even the most casual reader.

## BOCCA: THE TRAITOR AT MONTAPERTI

If Mosca provides the occasion for a study of the principal
cause of the political schism that pervades Dante's imagination, the encounter with Bocca degli Abati shows the effects.
Again demonstrating that politics in the *Inferno* is invariably
local, Dante explodes in an unexpected and violent frenzy when
he comes across Bocca in Cocytus, the ninth and last circle of
Hell. Dante's Cocytus is a vast frozen river divided into four areas that make concentric circles, each lower in the ice than the
former. Here we encounter the traitors, who are divided into
four groups. Each group is relegated to a different area: Caina, named after Cain, the biblical character who murdered his
brother, Abel, is reserved for traitors to kin; Antenora, named

after the Trojan Antenore, who betrayed his city to the Greeks, houses traitors to party and homeland; Ptolomea, named after Ptolemy, King of Jericho, who murdered Simon the Maccabee and his two sons at a banquet, holds those treacherous to guests; and Giudecca, named after Judas, the betrayer of Christ, contains traitors to benefactors.

We are now at the center of Earth and at the base of all sin. In line 8, Dante announces the subject of this canto as "the bottom of the whole universe." Cocytus contains the rabble of Earth, unredeemed humanity—violent sinners who prey on family, their community, guests, and benefactors. The traitors are embedded in the frozen river. The heads of the sinners protrude from the ice, as Dante quaintly puts it, like frogs lifting up their faces above the water in summer. The contrapasso is evident: This frigid punishment corresponds to the coldness of their premeditated acts of treachery, the coldness of their perfidious hearts.

As Dante and Virgil are walking from Caina toward Antenora, the pilgrim inadvertently steps on the head of one of the sinners.

> . . . whether it was will or fate or chance I do not know, but, walking among the heads, I struck my foot hard in the face of one.
>
> Wailing he railed at me, "Why do you trample on me? If you do not come to increase the vengeance of Montaperti, why do you molest me?"
>
> And I, "Master, now wait here for me, that I may rid me of a doubt respecting this one, then you shall make me hasten as much as you wish." My leader stopped; and I said to the shade who was still cursing bitterly, "Who are you that thus reproach another?" "Nay, who are you," he answered, "that go through Antenora smiting the cheeks of others, so that, were you alive, it would be too much."

"Alive I am," was my reply, "and if you crave fame, it may be worth much to you that I note your name among the rest." And he to me, "The contrary is what I crave. Take yourself hence and trouble me no more, for ill do you know how to flatter in this depth." Then I seized him by the hair of the nape and said, "Either you'll name yourself, or not a hair will be left on you here."

Whereon he said to me, "Though you strip me bald, I will not tell you or show you who I am, though you should fall a thousand times upon my head."

I had already twisted his hair in my hand and had yanked out more than one tuft, he barking and with his eyes kept close down, when another cried, "What ails you, Bocca? Is it not enough for you to make noise with your jaws, but you must bark? What devil is at you?"

"Now," said I, "I do not wish you to speak more, accursed traitor, for to your shame I will carry true news of you." (*Inf.* 32.75–111)

Dante has been dignified in the face of political enemies such as Farinata, reverential in his treatment of Brunetto, and courteous to the three Florentine sodomites. Here, though, passion consumes the pilgrim. Bocca degli Abati was a Florentine nobleman and Ghibelline. Although the Abati were a Ghibelline family, at Montaperti, Bocca fought as a Florentine Guelf. At the height of the battle, Bocca suddenly switched sides by cutting off the hand of the Florentine standard-bearer, creating panic among his Guelf comrades. This unexpected treachery made it easier for the Ghibellines to defeat the Guelfs. Although there was some debate at the time over the identity of the traitor at Montaperti, Dante leaves no doubt about who the betrayer was in his account.

Political violence frames this unusually physical encounter. Bocca initiates the action with an immediate reference to

Montaperti, and Dante seems determined to pursue "a doubt" about the traitor. There is no subtlety in the pilgrim's actions here, and there is no idle curiosity. Dante treats Bocca with a fury as cold as the ice of Caina. The pilgrim kicks him in the head, badgers him, and rips out clumps of his hair. The kick may have been accidental, but the interrogation that follows is deliberate. It has all the hallmarks of an aggressor trying to extract the information he wants from his victim by any means. Dante begins their exchange by rebuking Bocca's bad manners, then offers fame for a price—he wants Bocca's story and to know his name: Bocca answers rudely and divulges nothing. As Dante starts pulling Bocca's hair, he "barks" in pain, prompting another sinner to name him. The encounter ends with Dante rejoicing in his victory over Bocca. He has discovered the traitor at Montaperti and revels in the disclosure and the shame he will bring on Bocca.

Dante's violence surprises many readers—it is hardly the behavior one expects to witness on a journey to salvation. Dante functions here as an instrument of God's justice, responding with violence to the violent and treacherous. This encounter is the most fraught of all the meetings with the damned, exceeding even the heated exchange with Filippo Argenti. Politics does not get more personal than this. Buoso da Duera, another traitor to his party, is the one who names Bocca. Buoso, a Ghibelline, betrayed the Ghibelline captain Manfred before the Battle of Benevento. Entrusted to hold passes near Parma against the forces of Charles I of Anjou, who was leading the Guelfs, Buoso took a bribe and let the troops through. In all, of the 17 traitors to their party named in canto 32, 15 are Italians from Dante's time. The numbers speak for themselves: For Dante, the division between the Guelfs and Ghibellines led to heinous and repeated acts of treachery over the course of more than 100 years. At the "bottom of the whole universe" lies Satan, of course. But close to the author of all evil lie those whose treachery defined the political disasters of Dante's historical moment.

As Dante makes clear in the other two canticles, political division is not confined to Florence. Party strife plagued Italy, and indeed the entire western empire. Dante excoriates the leadership of both church and state. The German Hohenstaufen emperors, in preferring to remain closer to home rather than occupying the imperial seat in Rome, shirk their duties as secular rulers. In 1309, Pope Clement V transferred the seat of the papacy from Rome to Avignon, where it would remain for the next 68 years. As Dante laments in *Purgatory*, Italy is a "ship without a pilot" (*Purg.* 6.77), a conglomeration of city-states without a leader. With the ship of state tossing in high seas without direction and Florence torn asunder by the pride, envy, and avarice of its citizens, Dante's world provides him with ample opportunity to condemn his contemporaries.

Long-standing Florentine hatreds saturate politics in the *Inferno*. As the pilgrim proceeds on his journey, part of his transformation lies in his release from these preoccupations. In *Purgatory*, political discussions become more abstract and theoretical. In the bright light of *Paradise*, Beatrice helps orient Dante toward a broader conception of justice. But Dante gives full vent to his terrestrial frustrations and anger before he arrives at this wider view.

The force of Dante's politicization of the epic has resonated through time. So powerful is his fulmination against his political situation that subsequent writers have resurrected him or his verse form to address their own political circumstances. When Percy Bysshe Shelley, the British Romantic poet, wished to speak to the political unrest of 1819 in his "Ode to the West Wind," he used Dante's verse form, terza rima, to reach back across time to a poet he admired:

> Drive my dead thoughts over the universe
> Like withered leaves to quicken a new birth!
> And, by the incantation of this verse,

Scatter, as from an unextinguished hearth
Ashes and sparks, my words among mankind!
Be through my lips to unawakened earth
The trumpet of a prophecy!

Shelley pays tribute to Dante in many ways in these lines. The rhyme scheme of the *Divine Comedy*—aba bcb cdc—is a difficult one to keep up in English, so the choice to follow Dante comes at some cost. But most Dantesque here is Shelley's assuredly prophetic stance. As we'll see in chapter 8, where we discuss Dan Brown's *Inferno,* the tradition of ecstatic prophecy is taken up by the scientist Zobrist, who, like Shelley, both pays homage to and exploits Dante's *Divine Comedy.*

# Churchmen in Hell

Dante's harsh treatment of clerics in the *Inferno* surprises many modern readers. His outbursts often target prominent members of the medieval church, which had great power over the everyday lives of Christians. Not only could critics of the church be tried in civic courts, but they might also, like the Knights Templar in southern France, be suppressed and killed. Church officials decreed the Waldensians heretical in northern Italy, and France persecuted them mercilessly in the thirteenth century. Yet Dante spares no rank in the church in the *Inferno,* where popes are damned for abdication, simony, and heresy and where monks and friars figure prominently among the hypocrites.

Dante's condemnation of corrupt ecclesiasts could not be more pervasive. The first and last souls he meets in Hell are clerics. Churchmen appear in eight different regions of Hell—nine if we include the neutrals. We find clerics among the avaricious and prodigal, heretics, sodomites, simonists, barrators, hypocrites, schismatics, and traitors. Notably, almost all the damned clergy are Italians who died between 1258 and 1307—that is, Dante's contemporaries. (The only two exceptions are Caiaphas and Annas, the Jewish high priests involved in Christ's sentence and crucifixion, who appear among the hypocrites in canto 23.) Many committed their misdeeds in the 1290s. Again, we see Dante's immersion in events of his own time.

Readers familiar with recent sexual and financial abuse scandals in the Catholic Church might find Dante's treatment surprisingly perceptive. Some similarities seem unusually resonant: Pope Boniface VIII, by simply transferring a Florentine bishop known for sexual excess to Vicenza, anticipates the response of many American bishops to sexual abuse among their clergy. Our response, however, should go beyond surprise at Dante's boldness and farsightedness. Clergymen are prominent in the *Inferno,* and given the poet's abiding faith in the church, we might ask what led him to put such emphasis on corruption among clerics.

## HISTORICAL BACKGROUND

To understand Dante's treatment of the clergy, it helps to know something about his views on the relationship between the church and state. The poet took a very dim view of ecclesiasts who sought to assert their power over temporal affairs. He addresses this subject in *Purgatory* 16:

> Rome, which made the world good, was wont to have two Suns, which made visible both the one road and the other, that of the world and that of God. The one has quenched the other, and the sword is joined to the crook: and the one together with the other must perforce go ill—since joined, the one does not fear the other. (*Purg.* 16.106–112)

Here Dante takes up one of the most debated subjects of his time: The relative authority of pope and emperor. He does so in a typically indirect way, using highly symbolic language. The passage plays on Rome's two histories—as the seat of power in the Roman Empire and as the seat of papal authority under Catholicism. Rome conquered the world under Augustus Caesar and succeeding emperors. After the fall of the Roman Empire, the rise of the church made Rome central to Europe again. In the passage, Dante presents these two authorities—church and empire—as the two suns.

These two powers were once separate—the church was dominant in spiritual affairs; the emperor was dominant in the secular world. Dante laments the confusion of these realms. Taking a very different position from what ecclesiasts had been arguing, namely that papal authority supersedes temporal prerogative, Dante claims that each should be supreme in its own sphere. However, the sword, symbol of temporal authority, has joined the shepherd's crook, symbol of ecclesiastical authority. With each body trying to seize the power of the other, the inevitable result is evil.[1]

Dante identifies the exact moment at which these two realms became confused—the moment of eclipse. He connects the confusion with the sin of avarice and emphasizes just this point in *Inferno* 19, after Pope Nicholas III (1277–1280) reveals how he enriched his own family and speaks of the misdeeds of two of his successors, Boniface VIII (1294–1303) and Clement V (1305–1314). Barely containing his outrage at the desecration of the church by these avaricious popes, the pilgrim cries out, "Ah, Constantine, of how much ill was mother, not your conversion, but that dowry which the first rich Father took from you!" (*Inf.* 19.115–117).

The "ill" here refers to the so-called Donation of Constantine, a document written around 760 by a Roman cleric, according to which Emperor Constantine I transferred authority over Rome and the western part of the Roman Empire to Pope Sylvester I. Presented as an edict by Constantine himself, the Donation decreed that the emperor made the transfer out of gratitude for Pope Sylvester curing him of leprosy. Although the Italian humanist Lorenzo Valla would prove this document a forgery in the fifteenth century, Dante and his contemporaries considered it authentic. Until Valla's decisive intervention, popes eager to expand their authority exploited the Donation of Constantine as a powerful weapon to advance the claim that papal authority takes precedence over imperial authority.

Dante doesn't so much deplore the Donation itself as its terrible consequences. In his eyes, Constantine's action initiated a taste for rule over temporal matters. The extent to which subsequent popes exploited the Donation by extending its terms cannot be overestimated. About 1200, Pope Innocent III argued that Constantine intended to relinquish the Western Empire to the pope and declared that the miter, symbol of papal authority, took precedence over the crown, the symbol of imperial authority. Dante considers the Donation of Constantine nothing less than the foundational act underlying the greed of a papacy ever more intent on expanding its authority.

Over the course of the twelfth to fourteenth centuries, a number of popes sought to increase papal power through various decrees. Boniface VIII issued one of the most notorious documents—the 1302 *Unam Sanctam*. In this bull (the title of which translates as "toward one, holy, catholic and apostolic church"), Boniface asserted the predominance of spiritual over temporal rule, more specifically his authority over King Philip the Fair of France. The bull states that the pope possesses the authority to institute earthly power and to stand in judgment over it.[2] In short, it advances Boniface's claim to be the sole head of the Christian world. Popes also pursued a lively ground campaign, expanding their territorial holdings, which allowed them to increase their tax revenues. By the end of the thirteenth century, the Papal States stretched from Ceprano and the river

Liri in the south to Radicofani in the north, and included much of central Italy.[3]

Papal adventurism during the reigns of Boniface VIII, Clement IV, Clement V, and John XXII seemed limitless, ranging from dynastic conflicts, such as the fights Boniface VIII and John XXII picked with Philip the Fair of France and with Louis of Bavaria, to petty squabbles, such as Clement IV's order that the Bishop of Cosenza disinter Manfred's remains after the Battle of Benevento and scatter them outside the kingdom. Excommunication of enemies was extremely common. We are a long way from Dante's separate suns lighting different paths. The balance of powers implied in separate realms of influence has given way to papal aggression and confusion of purpose. Popes concern themselves too much with the things of this world—hence Dante's linking of misguided papal authority and avarice.

But it was not only papal intrusion into the secular path that concerned Dante. Ambitious kings could also seek to co-opt the pope. Another momentous event, the removal of the papal see from Rome to Avignon in 1309, fueled Dante's grave concerns about the church. Upon his election in 1305, Clement V (Bertrand de Got, the Archbishop of Bordeaux) moved the papal curia to France. A tool of the French monarchy, Clement V never even went to Rome, ruling first in Poitiers for four years before moving the entire papal court to Avignon. In the absence of the supreme pontiff, three cardinals ruled Rome, a city torn asunder by two powerful Roman families, the Orsini and the Colonna. Termed the Babylonian Captivity by the Italian poet Petrarch, the Avignon papacy lasted until 1376.

Over the course of Dante's life (1265–1321), 14 popes reigned. He mentions 9 in the poem, 5 of whom are in Hell. Dante mentions 73 ecclesiasts in the *Comedy:* 20 are named in the *Inferno,* 16 of whom are damned. He names 14 churchmen in *Purgatory* and 47 in *Paradise*. At first glance, one might conclude that there are more blessed churchmen in Heaven. However, a closer look at these 47 figures shows that the overwhelming majority are early Christian martyrs, saints, and scriptural commentators. Among the popes who ruled during his lifetime, Dante places only one, John XXI, in Paradise. Although Dante praises clerics of the past, he inveighs against many contemporary churchmen.

## A ROGUE'S GALLERY: CLERICAL MISDEEDS

From beginning to end, the *Inferno* is full of churchmen, and Dante goes out of his way to make their appearances memorable by employing a mix of surprise, mockery, and invective. What might have been a glum litany becomes a display of technical mastery as Dante enlivens his disdain for corrupt ecclesiasts with mordant humor and irony. Readers might enjoy Dante's panoramic account of clerical misdeeds simply for itself. But for our purposes, we might note that Dante's poem also functions as an encyclopedic resource for later attacks on the church. Dante is not the first writer to assail religious figures or priests, but he combines censure of specific churchmen with a more systematic account of ecclesiastical corruption.

Even before he enters Hell proper, Dante recognizes a former pope. In the area just inside the Gate of Hell, Dante sees the neutrals, cowardly souls too weak-minded to take a position in life. Their punishment recalls their moral failing: Those who never took a side in life run frantically after a banner—they assume a pose of commitment, finally, but that commitment is empty. They had the opportunity to take actions that mattered while alive; now they spend eternity in hectic but meaningless pursuit. Among them Dante recognizes the shade "who from cowardice made the great refusal" *(Inf.* 3.60). Dante's earliest commentators identified this unnamed individual as Pope Celestine V, who abdicated only five months after his election. In

Dante's mind, the consequences of this action were disastrous: Celestine V's abdication led to the appointment of Boniface VIII, one of the most reviled figures in the *Comedy*. Notwithstanding Celestine's devoutness, Dante damns him. In Dante's eyes, once summoned to such an office, one must rise to the call. Celestine's refusal of the highest religious office amounts to an abdication of a sacred duty.

Dante expected his contemporaries to be able to identify Celestine from his derisive indirect allusion: The terms "cowardice" and "great refusal" were enough to signal whom the poet had in mind to early readers. Dante's son, Pietro Alighieri, wrote in his commentary (ca. 1340) with a disdain that recalls that of his father: "I believe he places among them Frate Pietro Morrone, who is known as Pope Celestine V. He could have led as holy and spiritual a life in the papacy as in his hermitage: and yet, he pusillanimously renounced the papacy, which is the seat of Christ."[4]

Nevertheless, the fact that the refuser is unnamed offers later writers an ideal opportunity. One can always propose another candidate or redirect the imaginative force of Dante's creation to comment on another situation. Dan Brown makes his fascination with the cowardly neutrals evident in the epigraph to his *Inferno*—"The darkest places in Hell are reserved for those who maintain their neutrality in times of moral crisis." Although Brown mistakenly places the neutrals among the "darkest places in Hell," his error conveys something of the severity with which Dante treats them. Many of the damned have a majesty, despite the evil of their actions on Earth. The neutrals are contemptible, unnamed, and unworthy of a place in Dante's account. His disdain for the neutrals—who, after all, did no wrong—seems excessive, but that very excess tells us how highly Dante values action. One must act: Only the weakminded wait on the sidelines and bide their time to see who ends up the victor when times are fraught. Even bad action is preferable to nullity.

At times Dante doesn't even have to identify a person by some well-known action or attribute. Early readers recognized the soul identified among the heretics simply as "the Cardinal" (*Inf.* 10.120) as a reference to Cardinal Ottaviano degli Ubaldini, a powerful church leader and papal legate in Lombardy. Dante knew that using the literary device of substituting an epithet or appellative for a proper name would allow his readers to identify the man, since Ottaviano frequently was referred to as "the Cardinal" when he was alive. Epithets function in the same way today: Everyone knows that the "Bambino" or the "Babe" refers to Babe Ruth and that "A-Rod" refers to Alex Rodriguez. A well-known supporter of the Ghibelline party, Cardinal Ubaldini is reported to have declared "If the soul exists, I have lost mine a thousand times for the Ghibellines." Such sentiments would confirm his damnation as heretic in Dante's poem.

We find one of Dante's most scathing references to clerics in canto 15, which treats the violent against nature. Although the poet never mentions the particular sin punished in cantos 15 and 16 by name, commentators assume that this circle includes sodomites among the blasphemers and usurers.[5] During his encounter with his former teacher Brunetto Latini, Dante asks who else is punished there. Brunetto mentions two grammarians, Priscian and Francesco d'Accorso, and then adds, "and you could also have seen there, had you hankered for such scurf, him who was transferred by the Servant of Servants from Arno to Bacchiglione, where he left his sinfully distended muscles" (*Inf.* 15.110–114). In this scornful account, Dante alludes to Andrea de' Mozzi, Bishop of Florence (1287–1295) and member of an elite Florentine family. Mozzi's debauchery was so notorious that Boniface VIII (the "Servant of Servants") removed Mozzi from his bishopric in Florence and transferred him to Vicenza. Dante clinches the identification cleverly by identifying Florence and Vicenza respectively by the rivers which flow through them, the Arno and the Bacchiglione. The reference to Mozzi's "sinfully distended muscles" alludes directly to the fleshly nature of the sin punished. Andrea de' Mozzi died near the banks of the Bacchiglione River, the muscles of his body worn out by fornication.

Some references to corrupt ecclesiasts are more straightforward. In noting the heresy of Pope Anastasius II and Photinus, the hypocrisy of the biblical characters Caiaphas and Annas, and the treachery of Tesauro dei Beccheria, Dante merely names the individual and the sin briefly. After their meeting with Farinata, Dante and Virgil find themselves near the tomb of Anastasius II, who, as a heretical pope who denied the divinity of Christ, presents one of the more shocking examples of unbelief in the poem. (Even great writers err! Dante confuses the pope with the Byzantine emperor Anastasius I.) Among the hypocrites, the amazing sight of one of the souls crucified on the ground interrupts Dante's exchange with two contemporary friars. Catalano explains:

> That transfixed one you are gazing at counseled the Pharisees that it was expedient to put one man to torture for the people. He is stretched out naked across the way, as you see, and needs must feel the weight of each that passes; and in like fashion his father-in-law racked in this ditch, and the others of that council which was a seed of evil for those Jews. (*Inf.* 23.115–123)

Here Dante sees the arch-hypocrite, Caiaphas, the Jewish high priest under Pontius Pilate, who, while concealing private reasons, told the Hebrew priests that it would be better to sacrifice Jesus than for the whole nation to perish. Responding in this way, Caiaphas pretended to be more interested in the good of others. For such colossal hypocrisy, Caiaphas and his father-in-law, Annas, a joint high priest, suffer a greater punishment than the other hypocrites, who tread over those crucified on the ground.

Dante indicts Tesauro dei Beccheria as a traitor to his party in the same matter-of-fact way, noting simply that one "of the Beccheria whose gullet was slit by Florence" (*Inf.* 32.119–120). Tesauro was Bishop of Vallombrosa and papal legate to Alexander IV. Accused of conspiring with the exiled Ghibellines, Tesauro was beheaded by the Florentines. Figures such as Anastasius II, Caiaphas, and Tesauro add to the panoply of ecclesiasts damned in Hell. All betrayed their religious vocation. Instead of serving the church and the faithful, they espoused heretical notions, acted fraudulently, or meddled in temporal affairs.

Dante's denunciations of clerics can be literal and direct, but he can also employ considerable subtlety and variation in his attacks. In *Inferno* 22, among the barrators, Virgil asks one sinner, captured by devils as he sought relief from the boiling tar in which he is immersed, about other Italians punished in this part of Hell. The captive is Fra Gomita, a friar who worked for Nino Visconti, a Sardinian judge. The lively response—the story of Fra Gomita's sleazy activities as go-between—defines the sin of barratry with dispatch:

> "Who was that from whom you say you made an ill departure to come ashore?"
>
> And he answered, "That was Fra Gomita, he of Gallura, vessel of every fraud, who had his master's enemies in his hand, and did so deal with them that they all praise him for it. He took cash and dismissed them smoothly, as he says; and in his other affairs too he was no petty barrator, but sovereign. Don Michel Zanche of Logodoro keeps company with him, and in talking of Sardinia their tongues are never weary." (*Inf.* 22.79–90)

The slippery world of bribery is made vivid in Dante's account. Described as a receptacle fit for every fraud, Fra Gomita routinely releases his master's enemies for gold. No common swindler, he is a kingpin among grafters. This friar's activities could not be further removed from his clerical duties. Ultimately, Nino Visconti had him hanged. Dante paints a humorous portrait of Fra Gomita gabbing endlessly with his compatriot Michele Zanche about Sardinia. Boiling in thick tar, the barrators can barely breathe, but they continue to talk.

Dante also employs irony in his treatment of Fra Dolcino, head of a sect known as the Apostolic Brothers that advocated living simply, as in the early days of Christianity, the so-called apostolic times. Church officials unsurprisingly declared the sect's practices, which included the communal sharing of goods and women, heretical. Clement V ordered that Fra Dolcino and his followers be wiped out. Authorities pursued the friar and thousands of his followers to the hills between Novara and Vercelli. Foreseeing his death, Mohammed, another schismatic, tells Dante to advise Fra Dolcino to provide himself with a good supply of food if he hopes to ward off his pursuers.

> Tell Fra Dolcino, then, you who perhaps will see the sun before long, if he would not soon follow me here, so to arm himself with victuals that stress of snow may not bring victory to the Novarese, which otherwise would not be easy to attain. (*Inf.* 28.55–60)

This is a bleak bit of humor. Most of Fra Dolcino's followers died of starvation, and the friar himself was captured and burned at the stake.

Fra Alberigo is the last soul the poet encounters in Hell. Dante makes an extravagant presentation here, playing fast and loose with time in the poem. The pilgrimage is made in 1300, but Fra Alberigo died in 1307. Hence Dante the pilgrim is surprised to see him. But as the encounter unfolds, the puzzle becomes a way for Dante to make it clear how treacherous these sinners are. As Dante and Virgil walk across Ptolomea, the area of Cocytus reserved for those who betrayed guests, one soul cries out for help, asking if a traveler will remove the large chunk of ice that has formed across his eyes. Those who committed such beastly acts of treachery are not permitted an outlet for their pain. Their tears freeze as soon as they fall, forming a kind of visor in front of their eyes. As Dante approaches, Fra Alberigo identifies himself:

> "I am Fra Alberigo; I am he of the fruits from the evil garden, and here I am paid date for fig."
> "Oh," I said to him, "are you then dead already?"
> And he to me, "How my body may fare in the world above I have no knowledge. Such vantage has this Ptolomea that oftentimes the soul falls down here before Atropos sends it forth; and that you may more willingly scrape the glazen tears from my face, know that as soon as the soul betrays as I did, its body is taken from it by a devil who thereafter rules it until its time has all revolved. The soul falls headlong into this cistern, and perhaps the body of the shade that is wintering here behind me still appears above on earth . . ."
> (*Inf.* 33.118–135)

We've seen treacherous souls as the pilgrim makes his way across Cocytus. But Dante emphasizes the depth of perfidy here, showing how some souls are so treacherous that they are damned *even before they are dead*. Fra Alberigo's soul suffers the torments of Hell while a devil inhabits his body on Earth. This remarkable invention allows Dante to condemn souls without resorting to prophecy. This claim also shows one of the poet's most notable departures from the theology of his day—Christian doctrine decrees that one cannot know the state of a soul until the moment of death. Dante clearly does not believe anyone as treacherous as Fra Alberigo is capable of repentance.

Fra Alberigo, a member of a Guelf family of Faenza, was a Jovial Friar, whose members could marry and own homes and property. The official name of the group to which he belonged was the Order of the Army of the Blessed Virgin Mary. After pretending to be reconciled with a relative, Fra Alberigo had him and one of his sons killed at a banquet at the signal of "bring the fruit." After this savage murder, Italians coined a proverb, "*le male frutta di frate Alberigo*"—"the bad fruits of Fra Alberigo." Dante plays on this saying when the sinner says he trades figs for dates in Hell. Just as medievals considered the date to be a more valuable fruit than the fig, so the punishment allotted Fra Alberigo is greater than the dessert he served to his cousin. Dante was so outraged by this savagery that he refused to remove the ice from Fra Alberigo's eyes, noting that "to be rude to him was courtesy" (*Inf.* 33.150). Here the pilgrim becomes an instrument of God's justice: One does not honor requests of villainous traitors.

None of the accounts of damned churchmen we have just considered betray even a hint of sympathy. With the exception of Celestine V, all are in Lower Hell, many in the two lowest circles of Hell. Dante's disdain for these clerics could not be more apparent. He is outraged at the sight of Caiaphas, denounces Andrea de' Mozzi's seedy habits with a withering description, mocks Fra Gomita, and blasts all of the inhabitants of Genoa for having a citizen as treacherous as Fra Alberigo in their midst. He treats all with the contempt he thinks they deserve.

## CATALANO AND LODERINO:
## HYPOCRITICAL FRIARS

The punishment of the hypocrites provides one of the most extravagant and surreal of the contrapassi. Upon his arrival in this ditch, Dante sees:

> . . . a painted people who were going round with very slow
> steps, weeping and in their looks tired and overcome. They
> wore cloaks with cowls down over their eyes, of the cut that
> is made for the monks of Cluny, so gilded outside that they
> dazzle within, all of lead, and so heavy that those Frederick
> imposed were of straw. (*Inf.* 23.58–66)

Throughout Hell, souls have been naked and exposed. The
hypocrites are extravagantly clothed, wearing heavy cloaks
made of lead painted gold on the outside. Because of the weight
of the cloaks, the hypocrites walk very slowly in their ditch
of Malebolge—a mockery of ecclesiastical solemnity and dignity. The punishment is inspired by a questionable etymology
of the word "hypocrite," which Dante likely found in a medieval handbook, Uguccione da Pisa's *Magnae derivationes*
(Great Derivations): "*hypocrita* derives from *hyper,* above, and
*crisis,* gold, *gilt over,* for on the surface and externally he appears good, but within he is evil."[6] Although this is a mistaken
definition, it sparks a gorgeous invention. Dante improves on
Uguccione's definition considerably. Not only does the contrapasso succinctly render the sin—a glittering exterior that hides
a base interior—but it also suggests its effects on the sinners,
who must bear the weight of their duplicity and corruption.[7]

The cut of the lead cloaks provides another indictment.
Their conspicuous resemblance to those worn by the monks at
a famous Benedictine abbey in Cluny, France, adds to Dante's
ongoing condemnation of the clergy and their habits. Being
outfitted in costly lavish garments hardly befits ecclesiasts, who
should be pious and disdain showy display. The clergy own this
sin along with simony and avarice.

One of the souls, Catalano, identifies himself and a companion, Loderingo, as Jovial Friars.

> We were Jovial Friars, and Bolognese: I named Catalano,
> and he Loderingo, and by your city chosen together, as one

man alone is usually chosen, to maintain the peace; and we were such, that it still appears around the Gardingo. (*Inf.* 23.103–108)

After the Battle of Benevento, officials summoned Catalano and Loderingo to Florence to represent the concerns of both political parties and make peace accords. However, the two friars sided with the winning party, the Guelfs. Catalano notes that one site in particular, Gardingo, gives evidence of their hypocrisy. Today this is the area around the Palazzo Vecchio in Florence. In Dante's time, the Uberti, one of the leading Ghibelline families, had their homes there. After Catalano and Loderingo's duplicitous dealings, the Guelfs destroyed the Uberti's properties, including the tower of Gardingo. Hence this blighted site stands as proof of the two friars' hypocrisy. The episode also entwines Dante's chief concerns—clerical corruption and political faction—in one infernal encounter.

## AVARICIOUS AND PRODIGAL CHURCHMEN

Dante condemns individual churchmen in various ways. He also presents clerics in groups, associating them pointedly with specific sins—notably avarice, simony, and hypocrisy. The fourth circle, where Dante and Virgil come across the avaricious and the prodigal, contains a host of clergymen.

As does the wave, there over Charybdis, breaking itself against the wave it meets, so must the folk here dance their round. Here I saw far more people than elsewhere, both on the one side and on the other, howling loudly, rolling weights, which they pushed with their chests; they clashed together, and then right there each wheeled round, rolling back on his weight, shouting, "Why do you hoard?" and "Why do you squander?" Thus they returned along the gloomy circle on either hand to the opposite point, shouting at each other again their reproachful refrain; then, having reached that point, each turned back through his half-circle to the next joust.

And I, heart-wrung at this, said, "Master, now declare to me who are these people, and if all these tonsured ones on our left were clerics."

And he to me, "Each and all of these were so asquint of mind in the first life that they followed there no right measure in their spending; most clearly do they bark this out when they come to the two points of the circle where opposite fault divides them. These who have no covering of hair on their head were clerics, and popes and cardinals, in whom avarice wreaks its excess." (Inf. 7.22–48)

Dante devotes considerable time to this spectacle. The avaricious, on the left, and the prodigal, on the right, push enormous heavy weights with their chests in a circle. When they meet at the halfway point of the circle, they clash, return, and begin the cycle again. Dante sardonically compares their movements to a dance and a joust, but it is a dance with no pleasure and a joust with no victor. We have only endless clashing. He likens the thunderous sound to the crashing waves that break over the classical whirlpool Charybdis, located near the Strait of Messina, the tumultuous place where the Ionian and Mediterranean seas meet between Sicily and the Italian mainland.

The punishment is one of Dante's finest conceptions. The weights suggest, on one level, the sinner's attachment to (or disregard of) material goods and money. Yet the symbol here is empty—a reminder of the vanity of this pursuit (or its disavowal). The punishment recalls that of Sisyphus in the classical tradition. Condemned to push a rock up a hill in Hades, Sisyphus completes his task only to see the rock roll back down. He is locked into an endless cycle of useless yet strenuous activity. Dante's analysis of the sins of avarice and prodigality operates at a deeper level as well, finding a likeness beneath superficial differences. The avaricious person clearly hoards money.

Dante, however, considers the prodigals similarly culpable since they spend without any sense of moderation, often dissipating carelessly their families' fortunes. The sin, ultimately, is neither hoarding nor spending: It lies in the misunderstanding of one's relation to material goods.

Dante develops this contrapasso with notable energy. Every detail becomes meaningful. When, following the pattern set in earlier encounters, Dante asks to speak to individual sinners, Virgil rebuffs him: "You harbor a vain thought: the undiscerning life that made them foul now makes them dim to all discernment" (*Inf.* 7.52–54). Such are the consequences of their lack of discernment: Those who did not distinguish properly in life are now indistinguishable in death. The uselessness of their actions in Hell mirrors the former futility of their lives, hoarding and spending indiscriminately.

Dante painstakingly identifies the clergy with avarice. On one level his anticlerical thrust coincides with a well-established tradition. Although Christ had led his followers in embracing poverty, and mendicant orders in the Middle Ages took vows of poverty, many medieval writers associated the clergy with greed. Chaucer (ca. 1343–1400) mocks the Pardoner, Summoner, and the Prioress in the *Canterbury Tales*. Superficially, the pilgrim's discovery of so many clerics in this circle—men supposedly above the allure of worldly goods—is both amusing and historically appropriate. Many clerics in Dante's time lived like princes. But the poet's purpose here goes deeper than simple outrage at churchmen. He structures his criticism of the church carefully: The church's exploitation of the Donation of Constantine, in Dante's eyes, led to a disastrous confusion of temporal and spiritual realms.

## SIMONY: THE SIN OF POPES

Distressed as he is by the propensity of the clergy to hoard and waste material goods, Dante reserves his greatest outrage for the sin of simony, the trafficking in spiritual goods. This practice ranges from selling the offices and benefices in the church, to granting indulgences and other ecclesiastical favors for money. Again Dante ultimately looks beyond the sin itself to address a deeper issue: the relation between church and state. The confusion of the two powers, especially the church's usurpation of the duties of the state, becomes his focus in *Inferno* 19.

The canto begins abruptly with Dante the poet praising the justness of the punishment in language that echoes the apocalyptic tone of the Last Judgment. Dante continues this elevated tone by tracing the sin back to its namesake, Simon Magus, who is first mentioned in Acts. A sorcerer from Samaria, Simon Magus became a Christian and then tried to buy the apostles' power of bestowing the Holy Spirit. For Dante, this sin, exclusive to churchmen and above all to popes, is especially reprehensible since it contaminates the world's spiritual leadership. Clerics ought to promote righteousness, not purvey corruption.

A description of the punishment, one of the most memorable in *Inferno*, begins in line 22:

> From the mouth of each projected the feet of a sinner and his legs as far as the calf, and the rest was within. They all had both their soles on fire, because of which their joints were twitching so hard that they would have snapped ropes and withes. As flame on oily things is wont to move only on their outer surface, so it did there, from the heels to the toes.
> (*Inf.* 19.22–30)

The punishment combines horror and humor to capitalize on the notion of inversion. Upside-down and writhing comically, in Hell these clergymen lose all the dignity of their office. When Dante first approaches Nicholas III, he jocularly distinguishes him as the sinner "who was lamenting with his shanks," hardly a flattering memorial. But this sight gag does not exhaust the possibilities for inversion in Dante's presentation. Those who corrupted the inheritance of St. Peter (notably described by Christ in a pun on his name as "the Rock" of the church) and pocketed wealth are themselves bagged or pursed in the bedrock of Hell. Commentators have also noted a parodic inversion of pentecostal fire in the punishment. The Holy Spirit descended as flames upon the heads of the apostles at Pentecost. Here flames play about the feet of the simonists.[8]

Dante often presents the symbolic framework of the contrapasso early in each encounter, in part to build toward a dramatic climax. *Inferno* 19 does this spectacularly. The poet notices that the flames burn one sinner more intensely than the others. When the sinner senses someone above his hole, he cries out:

> Are you already standing there, are you already standing there, Bonifazio? By several years the writ has lied to me. Are you so quickly sated with those gains for which you did not fear to take by guile the beautiful Lady, and then do her outrage? (*Inf.* 19.52–57)

Here Dante manages to skewer two clerics with one quip. First and foremost, the poet condemns Boniface VIII, who as pope (1294–1303) supported Dante's political enemies, the Black Guelfs. The speaker is another pope, Nicholas III, whom Dante roundly denounces as a simonist and nepotist while in office (1277–1280). (See figure 4.) The humor comes in two ways: from our surprise at a pope expecting another pope and from Dante's clever manipulation of time to predict Boniface's future damnation. Upside-down and unable to see, Nicholas is furious when he thinks he's misread the book of the future, for he believes that the man standing before him is none other than his successor, Boniface VIII.

In this episode, Dante again exploits his strategy of setting the journey in 1300. By placing the action of the poem in the

Fig. 4.   Gustave Doré, *Punishment of Nicholas III,* Courtesy of the
Division of Rare and Manuscript Collections, Cornell University Library.

past, he can predict the future—that is, a future that, by the
time he writes the *Inferno,* he already knows. Dante can condemn Boniface VIII, the man he held responsible for his exile
and reviled for many other nefarious activities. In *Inferno 6,*
Ciacco alluded to Boniface's support of the Blacks who gained
reentry into Florence in 1302. In this canto, Dante focuses on
the pope's simony. Nicholas III alludes to Boniface's fraudulent

seizure of the wealth of the church (i.e., the "Lovely Lady," the church as the Bride of Christ). The accusation of taking the church by "guile" likely refers to Boniface's machinations (according to contemporary chroniclers) to have himself elected pope after the abdication of Celestine V.

Seeing that Dante is stunned into silence by Nicholas's misidentification of him as Boniface, Virgil urges the pilgrim to say "I am not he." Nicholas must now confess his own sins, which occasions another comic inversion. Dante now becomes the confessor to the pope—a witty reversal of church ritual. Dante also plays on the common medieval practice of punishing assassins by burying them upside-down to suffocate them slowly. Nicholas takes the position of communicant, confessing various sins, as well as that of convicted assassin. The pope's confession allows Dante further comic possibilities as the poet plays on Nicholas's last name, Orsini, which shares the same root as "*orso,*" Italian for "bear." The pope informs Dante that "as a son of the she-bear," he eagerly advanced the "cubs," his own family. Nicholas himself notes the irony of his predicament. Finally, even Nicholas seems to participate in the cruel levity of Dante's puns and witticisms. He notes that, in life, he pursed ill-gotten wealth: In Hell, he is literally pursed in the bedrock.

The humor of this scheme—pope replacing pope in a humiliating series—should not blind us to the seriousness of Dante's charges. When Boniface VIII arrives, he will push Nicholas III farther down into the crevice, just as Boniface's successor will stuff him farther down. Nicholas then predicts the arrival of Boniface's successor, Clement V, who was elected pope in 1305.

> I shall be thrust down there in my turn when he comes for
> whom I mistook you when I put my sudden question. But
> longer already is the time that I have cooked my feet and
> stood inverted thus than he shall stay planted with glowing

feet, for after him shall come a lawless shepherd from the west, of uglier deeds, one fit to cover both him and me. A new Jason he will be, like him we read of in Maccabees, but even as to that one his king was pliant, so to this one shall be he who governs France. (*Inf.* 19.76–88)

While Boniface and Nicholas are severely condemned, Dante considers Clement V's offenses greater. Nicholas characterizes Clement V's actions as unbridled and outrageous, likening them to those of Jason, brother of the high priest Onias III, who obtained the office of high priest from the King of Syria, Antiochus IV Epiphanes (ca. 175 B.C.) through bribes. Just as Jason won his office through corruption, so does Clement V owe his appointment to another king, Philip the Fair of France.[9]

Dante makes no effort to conceal his disgust with three of the popes of his time. He lambasts Nicholas III, Boniface VIII, and Clement V for a host of despicable and irreligious activities—fomenting a rebellion in Sicily against Charles of Anjou, engineering one's own election to the papacy, colluding with foreign monarchs, and enriching one's own relations. Little wonder that the pilgrim cannot contain his outrage and deplores such sacrilege in a bitter rant. Their "avarice afflicts the world" (*Inf.* 19.104). They have prostituted the goods of the church, turning it into the whore of Babylon decried in the Bible. Tellingly, he concludes with a denunciation of the evil effects of the Donation of Constantine, the root, for Dante, of all this evil.

## BONIFACE VIII: THE HEIGHTS OF INFAMY

The last allusion to Boniface occurs in *Inferno* 27. Here Dante meets Guido da Montefeltro, the lord of Urbino, who is condemned as a false counselor (i.e., for employing his intelligence or eloquence to deceive others). One cannot, of course, separate false counsel from speech, and Dante exploits this connection through a highly poetic link. The sinners are imprisoned in flames—literally tongues of flames—which makes speech excruciating for them. What was so easy before, their eloquent and persuasive discourse, becomes their eternal torment.

Guido da Montefeltro was a Ghibelline general famed for his skill as a military commander and tactician. According to a contemporary chronicle, Guido was "the shrewdest and finest soldier that there was in Italy at that time."[10] Leader of the Ghibelline forces in Romagna and the head of many campaigns against the Guelfs and papal armies, Guido was excommunicated by the church. Nevertheless, after a reconciliation, he ended his life in 1298 as a Franciscan monk (the "corded friar" to which Guido alludes in line 69). His candor is beguiling. He indicates, with some pride, that his actions as soldier were not those of the lion—physical feats of daring—but those of the fox—cunning and sagacity. Guido distinguished himself not on the battlefield but from the command post, by scheming and deceit. His contemporaries feared and admired his shrewdness and treachery in battle. One chronicler observed: "when Count Guido came out of Pisa, the Florentines would flee saying: 'here comes the fox.'"[11]

Guido describes the circumstances that led to his damnation in one of the longest confessions in the *Inferno*:

I was a man of arms, and then a corded friar, trusting, so girt, to make amends; and certainly my hope would have come full, but for the High Priest—may ill befall him!—who set me back in my first sins: and how and wherefore I would have you hear from me. While I was the form of the flesh and bones my mother gave me, my deeds were not those of the lion, but of the fox. I knew all wiles and covert ways, and plied the art of them so well that to the ends of the earth their sound went forth. When I saw myself come to that part of my life when every man should lower the sails and coil up the ropes, that which before had pleased me grieved me then, and with repentance and confession I turned friar, and—woe is me!—it would have availed.

The Prince of the new Pharisees, having war near the Lateran—and not with Saracens or with Jews, for his every enemy was Christian, and none had been to conquer Acre, nor been a merchant in the Soldan's land—regarded neither the supreme office and holy orders in himself, nor, in me, that cord which used to make its wearers leaner; but as Constantine sought out Sylvester within Soracte to cure his leprosy, so this one sought me out as the doctor to cure the fever of his pride. He asked counsel of me, and I kept silent, for his words seemed drunken. Then he spoke again, "Let not your heart mistrust. I absolve you here and now, and do you teach me how I may cast Penestrino to the ground. I can lock and unlock Heaven, as you know; for the keys are two, which my predecessor did not hold dear." Thereon the weighty arguments pushed me to where silence seemed to me the worst, and I said, "Father, since you do wash me of that sin into which I now must fall, long promise with short keeping will make you triumph on the High Seat." (*Inf.* 27.67–111)

Guido's speech is a tour de force. The false counselor is himself undone by false counsel—by the combined force of Boniface's treacherous religious advice and his own overestimation of his own cunning. Dante compounds the ironies by pointing out another failure on Guido's part: The sinner does not understand the nature of the pilgrim's presence in Hell. Guido speaks to Dante under the assumption that Dante is dead—hence unable to harm Guido's reputation on Earth, where people would believe him saved by his late entry into the Franciscan order. Of course Dante is only too happy to include Guido's confession of his perfidy in the *Inferno*.

In lines 85 to 111, Guido describes his dealings with Boniface, again in the blackest of terms, referring to him as "the Prince of the new Pharisees" (85). As Guido reveals, Boniface pays a visit to him at the monastery in order to lure the old fox out of retirement and obtain his advice for one last campaign. The pope had been waging war against the Colonna family, which had contested the legitimacy of his election, and wants to know how to storm their fortress at Penestrina. Even Guido realizes Boniface's evil. This is no crusade. Boniface is not fighting infidels: He's waging a war of Christians against Christians, a war without justification, a personal vendetta.

Guido's tortured confession is one of the high points in the poem. In lines 94 to 96, Guido likens Boniface's approach to Constantine's seeking out of Pope Sylvester on Mount Soracte. Readers at once sense the complexity of such a gesture—a loaded comparison, given Dante's hostility to the Donation of Constantine. Pope Sylvester reputedly cured Constantine of a real ailment, leprosy. Guido, as physician to Boniface, addresses a metaphorical fever, the pope's mad desire to wipe out the Colonna. The comparison serves to emphasize the difference between these cures. Moreover, Dante hardly intends to flatter Boniface with this reference. The poet likens Boniface to Constantine as a *temporal,* not a religious, figure.

The ironies here could not be sharper. The bait that Boniface dangles in front of Guido is absolution—"I can lock and unlock Heaven, as you know," the pope cunningly assures the wily Guido. Boniface offers to absolve the general in advance of any sin he may commit. One imagines the calculation here, as Guido, mindful of Boniface's delirium, his frenzy for blood, as well as his obvious misuse of his power in offering absolution in advance, weighs the offer. Guido ends his silence, urging Boniface, with a terseness that belies the enormity of the consequences, to employ "long promise with short keeping." In other words, Guido advises the pope to behave fraudulently—make

long-term pledges, then break them. Boniface entered the fortified town of Palestrina with false promises of amnesty. Once
in possession of the town, Boniface ordered it razed. Boniface
betrays Guido, as he does the inhabitants of Palestrina, with
false assurances.

At the end of the canto, Dante takes puckish delight in re-
staging the fox's damnation, as a devil intercepts St. Francis,
who has come to collect Guido, and claims his soul for Hell.
The devil seizes upon Guido with a stinging witticism, as he
taunts "Perhaps you did not think that I was a logician!" (*Inf.*
27.122–123). For one cannot repent and sin at once. By know-
ingly planning to sin and at the same time be absolved of his
sin, Guido attempts the ultimate deception: He tries to defraud
God and divine justice. The false counselor provides false counsel to himself.


## A DURABLE HATRED

As one might expect, Dante's denunciation of the clergy is not
confined to the *Inferno*. In *Purgatory,* Dante examines the roles
of church and state from a more philosophical perspective. He
provides a scathing condemnation of the desecration of the
church at the top of the mountain of Purgatory. There the pilgrim witnesses a dramatic series of transformations of a chariot
that represents the church, an allegorical pageant that portrays
successive outrages, including the Donation of Constantine.

St. Peter offers a final perspective in *Paradiso* 27 when he
denounces his corrupt successors in a fierce invective:

> The spouse of Christ was not nurtured on my blood and
> that of Linus and of Cletus, to be employed for gain of
> gold . . . Rapacious wolves, in shepherd's garb, are seen from
> here above in all the pastures: O defense of God, wherefore
> dost thou yet lie still? Cahorsines and Gascons make ready

to drink our blood. O good beginning, to what vile ending
must you fall! But the high Providence, which with Scipio defended for Rome the glory of the world, will succor speedily,
as I conceive. . . . (*Par.* 27.40–42; 57–63)

Even from so lofty a perspective, Dante takes care to emphasize
the local and the contemporary amid his litany of papal excess,
corruption, and irreligiosity. Peter laments the desecration of his
inheritance by rapacious popes all too ready to drink his blood
and that of early martyrs, such as Linus and Cletus (respectively
the second and third popes). He singles out for condemnation
the Gascons and Cahorsines, references to the birthplaces of
Clement V and his successor, John XXII. Yet there is also hope
in Peter's final words: He foresees divine intervention and the
renewal of the glory of the world.

# Hell on Earth

## Dante's Treatment of Place

Dante, writing the *Inferno*, is essentially homeless. He describes his situation in plaintive language in *Paradiso*, when his ancestor Cacciaguida predicts the pilgrim's future:

> You shall leave everything beloved most dearly; and this is the arrow which the bow of exile shoots first. You shall come to know how salt is the taste of another's bread, and how hard the path to descend and mount by another man's stairs. (*Par.* 17.55–60)

Such complaints are extremely concrete, even visceral. Dante expresses his loss in terms of taste—the homely texture of his daily bread—and motion, in the monotony of going up and down. Exile makes familiar, everyday acts bitter.

During the years of his exile, Dante wandered much of northern and central Italy. Although his exact movements are uncertain, according to Giovanni Boccaccio, author of the *Decameron* and Dante's first biographer, Dante's travels may have taken him as far as Paris. These wanderings provided Dante with much of the raw material for his poem. We can imagine him gathering stories while the guest of rulers and lords in Verona, Forlì, Romena, Ravenna, and Venice. We can also imagine Dante gathering the visual detail that enriches the poem—details such as the description of the optical illusion created by the two towers of Bologna (*Inf.* 31.136–45) or perhaps the virtuoso account of the Arsenal in Venice, with its bustling repair of ships (*Inf.* 21.7–22). In 1892 Mary Hensman, a devoted student of Dante, created the Dante Map, a fascinating bit of cartography that shows all the places in Italy mentioned by Dante in the *Comedy* in one font and all the places that Dante passed through during his exile in another.[1] Nineteenth-century travelers taking the Grand Tour would visit these places, avidly following in the great poet's footsteps, whether historical or traditionary. Such pilgrimages, whether acts of reverence or simply tourism, testify to the descriptive force of Dante's poem.

But while the brute detail of the pains of exile in Dante's poem is memorable, equally powerful are his more abstract accounts. In the *Convivio,* a philosophical treatise Dante wrote while moving from place to place, the poet laments

> Since it was the pleasure of the citizens of the most beautiful and famous daughter of Rome, Florence, to cast me out of her sweet bosom . . . I have traveled like a stranger, almost a beggar, through virtually all the regions to which this tongue of ours extends, displaying against my will the wound of fortune for which the wounded one is often unjustly accustomed to be held accountable. (*Convivio,* 1.4–5)

Both the tone and the subtlety of this passage merit close consideration. Dante combines sarcasm with genuine affection, and he juxtaposes the action of fortune with that of justice. It is not simply the punishment of exile that rankles—the climbing of others' stairs or the bitter taste of others' bread—it is the sense that others might find the punishment to be fitting. In the world that the exiled Dante moves through, the punishment need not fit any crime, unlike in the *Inferno,* where the law of contrapasso ensures it.

T. S. Eliot, a twentieth-century poet and critic who often turned to Dante's poem for inspiration, provides a useful discussion of this split between thought and concrete detail in Dante. In a 1921 essay with the spare title "Dante," Eliot insists that part of the poet's job as that of "trying to *realize* ideas" as opposed to the more philosophical task of "deal[ing] with ideas in themselves."[2] This focus on the means of expression as a process is suggestive. Eliot expands on this notion in a later essay published in 1929, this one simply titled "Inferno," in which he insists not only on Dante's preference for "clear visual images" but also the poet's "*visual* imagination." Eliot puts it another way later in the same essay: "Dante attempts to make us see what he saw."[3]

In a sense, Eliot simply restates the obvious. Hell's varied landscapes have long fascinated readers. Classical writers established basic topographical features of some places in Hell, along with the idea of varied punishments, and the persistence of this tradition suggests its appeal. While Dante follows Ovid and Virgil in his inclusion of the four rivers of Hell—the Acheron, Styx, Phlegethon, and Cocytus—he manipulates these borrowings, transforming them in striking ways. By turning each of the rivers into a place of specific punishment—murderers, tyrants, and plunderers boiling in Phlegethon, now a river of blood; the wrathful writhing in the muddy swamp of Styx; traitors freezing in the frozen lake of Cocytus—Dante provides the "clear visual image" Eliot praises as fundamental to the poem. And that, no doubt, is enough for enjoying the poem. But Eliot's remarks go further. To "realize," as Eliot puts it, an idea (like the contrapasso) as one of these "clear visual images" is to concentrate and redouble the force of the poem. Eliot reminds us that Dante's *making*—that is, the process of realizing his idea—is important as well as spectacle. Dante, as he writes his poem, is placeless, yet he bends the *Divine Comedy* to an intense consideration of place.

## VISUALIZING THE LANDSCAPE OF HELL

In a poem of 14,232 lines, Dante refers to 125 historical places, a fairly dense count for a poem that concerns the underworld. These references are rare in the first five circles of Hell—Dante mentions Italy, Rome, Florence, and Rimini—and are fairly straightforward. For instance, when Dante mentions Rome in *Inferno* 2.20–24, he does so to organize readers' thoughts about the city along two lines: as the seat of the Roman Empire and the classical literary tradition, and subsequently as the seat of the Catholic Church. The name "Rome" can conjure up many ideas and associations, but Dante restricts these to the two that suit his poem. Later, in *Inferno* 5, Francesca uses place as a graceful indication of her homeland. She is from the place where the Po River "descends to be at peace" (*Inf.* 5.99) in the sea, Rimini. The reference locates Francesca, and it allows her to contrast the peaceful descent of the river and her present situation, in which winds pummel those damned for lust.

The use of place becomes more complicated as the poem develops. Dante increasingly compares places in Hell to locales on Earth not only to help readers imagine the unimaginable—to "make us see what he saw," as Eliot puts it—but also to remind us of their differences. We find the first example of such a comparison just after Dante and Virgil enter Dis, the walled city of Lower Hell. Upon entering the sixth circle, which houses the heretics, Dante sees a vast landscape of burning tombs. He compares the landscape to two ancient Roman burial places.

> . . . on every hand I see a great plain full of woe and of cruel torment. As at Arles, where the Rhone slackens its course, and as at Pola, near the Quarnero, which shuts Italy in and bathes her borders, the sepulchers make all the place uneven, so they did here on every side, save that the manner here was more bitter; for among the tombs, flames were scattered, whereby they were made to glow all over . . . (*Inf.* 9.110–119)

This is a particularly sharp visual image. Dante mentions the large stone tombs at Arles in southern France (see figure 3), and Pola, another Roman necropolis on the Istrian peninsula, taking care to mention bodies of water near these two sites. Readers who have visited these sites or seen images of them can better imagine the size and nature of the tombs. Yet the *Inferno* tombs also differ notably from the stone sarcophagi of the Romans. The dead here do not rest, they burn.

There are many other examples of this kind of geographical comparison. For example, Dante compares the wood of the suicides to Cecina and Corneto, areas of savage wilderness in thirteenth-century Tuscany, noting that these bleak places do not compare to the "rough" and "dense" wood of the suicides (*Inf.* 13.7–9). Similarly, he notes that an area of tumbled rocks in the seventh circle resembles the aftermath of a landslide near Trent (*Inf.* 12.4–6), that the red rivulet that runs through the burning plain of that circle resembles the Bulicame, a hot sulfurous spring near Viterbo, and that the frozen ice of Cocytus surpasses the hardness of the Danube and Don rivers when frozen. These are simple and effective answers to the questions of how rugged, how red, how hot, or how hard. But while the comparisons make the strange infernal world more familiar, in each case we might note that Hell exceeds description, no matter how suggestive the means of description might be.

## FLORENCE IN HELL

Dante's attitude toward Florence is predictably complex. His remarks in the *Convivio* make clear that Florence can be at once a "sweet bosom" for which the exile pines as well as the city whose citizens cast him out and branded him unjustly. Dante refers to Florence more than any other place in the *Comedy*—approximately 31 times. As in his treatment of people, Dante also employs circumlocutions, roundabout expressions to refer to the city. Among the positive allusions, we have Farinata's designation of Florence as a "noble fatherland" (*Inf.* 10.26); an anonymous Florentine suicide's allusion to "the city that changed her first patron for the Baptist" (*Inf.* 13.143–44); and Dante the pilgrim's reference to Florence as a "great town" (*Inf.* 23.95) through which the "fair stream of Arno" flows, when talking to the hypocrites. Dante's and Farinata's statements reveal great civic pride, while the Florentine suicide provides some historical background: In ancient times, Mars was the city's patron, but later John the Baptist replaced him. In another passage, Dante mentions one of the city's most famous buildings, the Baptistry, affectionately termed "my beautiful San Giovanni" (*Inf.* 19.17), the site of the poet's baptism. Despite his exile, Dante clearly retains positive memories of his native city and expresses his affection for Florence through the pilgrim and other characters.

Other indirect expressions are more critical. The glutton Ciacco characterizes Florence as a "divided city" (*Inf.* 6.61) and a place "so full of envy that already the sack runs over" (*Inf.* 6.49–50). Brunetto Latini refers to the town as "the nest of so much wickedness" (*Inf.* 15.77), and one of the Florentine sodomites describes it as a "degenerate city" (*Inf.* 16.9). Taken together, these positive and negative expressions reveal Dante's love-hate relationship with Florence. But these evocations of place also frame a long series of formal considerations of particular cities. As Dante the pilgrim grows more familiar with the order of the underworld city of Dis, he begins to organize his presentation of cities on Earth. Hell, for the pilgrim as well as the poet, is a judgment on places as well as people, and many of these judgments fall on cities. The infernal city has a terrestrial counterpart.

## SIN CITIES

Florence, as Dante's hometown, is in a category of its own, but it is by no means Dante's only target. After Dante enters Lower Hell, he expands his critique of corrupt places to include many other towns. He mocks Bologna as a place full of pimps and panderers, Siena for the frivolity of its citizens, and Lucca as a hotbed for graft. He blasts Pistoia, Pisa, and Genoa for the horrific crimes perpetrated there.

In order to clarify what is unusual about Dante's use of place, let us first look at some of his more ordinary references to cities. In *Inferno* 11, Virgil explains the division of Hell's sins to the pilgrim. The canto, often considered the plan of Hell canto, clarifies Dante's notion of justice. In his explanation of the sins punished in the seventh circle, Virgil identifies and classifies three groups of violent sinners: blasphemers, sodomites, and usurers. Interestingly, he clarifies the sins against nature by referring to two cities.

> Violence may be done against the Deity, by denying and blaspheming Him in the heart, and despising Nature and her goodness; and therefore the smallest ring seals with its mark both Sodom and Cahors, and all who speak contemning God in their heart. (*Inf.* 11.46–51)

The Book of Genesis describes Sodom, an ancient city of Palestine, as a den of iniquity—infamous enough to provide the word for the deed. God destroyed Sodom extravagantly by fire and brimstone. In Dante's time, Cahors, a town in southern France, was famous for the practice of usury (lending money with interest). Dante classifies usury as a crime against nature, a violation of more honest forms of moneymaking and human industry. Usury draws profit from something unnatural—money. Presumably, the reference would be familiar to Dante's readers, who would perform the simplest act of interpretation—a decoding. Even here, however, the poet cannot avoid a bit of flamboyance: The coupling of Sodom and Cahors, essentially putting them on equal footing as indices, reinforces one of his key points in the poem—that the providential history of Christianity, made manifest by the journey through Hell, tends to collapse differences in time. But the reference is nevertheless straightforward.

Other passages make far more ornate references. Dante's vilification of Lucca as a hotbed of graft combines broad humor and puzzling indirection. Never one to do anything so banal as to declare baldly that Lucca is full of corrupt public officials, Dante evokes the city in imaginative ways. The use of colloquial expressions, vivid animal comparisons, and the farcical behavior of the inhabitants of this ditch all contribute to the boisterous tone. The barrators seethe in black tar, ever on the lookout to escape the punishment. Whenever this happens, mayhem ensues, as the Malebranche, or Evil Claws—Dante's name for the demonic enforcers who patrol the ditch—hunt down the escapees, then torture them gleefully. Lines 38 to 42 highlight Dante's association of Lucca with the sin of barratry:

> He spoke from our bridge, "O Malebranche, here's one
> of Saint Zita's Elders! Thrust him under, while I go back for
> more, to that city where there's a fine supply of them: every

man there is a barrator, except Bonturo, there they make *Ay*
of *No*, for cash."

    Down he hurled him, and turned back on the hard crag,
and never was an unleashed mastiff so swift in pursuit of a
thief. The sinner sank under and rose again, rump up; but the
devils, who were under cover of the bridge, cried, "Here's no
place for the Holy Face! Here you'll swim otherwise than in
the Serchio! And so, unless you want to feel our grapples, do
not come out above the pitch." (*Inf.* 21.37–51)

Such a passage requires far more than simple decoding. Part
of the pleasure of this comic interlude lies in the fact that we
must puzzle it out. There is playfulness here, as Dante allows us
gradually to understand his presentation. One of the devils mer-
rily announces that he has just caught an elder of Santa Zita, a
boast that immediately identifies his captive as Lucchese. Lucca
adopted Zita (1218–ca.1278) as its patron saint after this maid-
servant's lifetime of faithful service. One of the Malebranche
informs his cohorts that Lucca is blessed with "a fine supply,"
adding sarcastically that everyone is on the take except one Bonturo. The corrupt head of the popular party in Lucca, Bonturo
was the most notorious grafter in Lucca. The quip implies that
all public officials in Lucca are corrupt—Bonturo bought and
sold public offices on so grand a scale that he virtually controlled
all trafficking in the city. In Lucca, all one needs to change a no
to a yes is lots of ready cash. As soon as he is released, the Lucchese barrator makes a beeline for the tar, hurling himself into
the pitch. When he surfaces, the devils prick him all over with
their prongs. The scene teems with violent and raucous activity.
In taunting their hapless victim further, the devils shout "Here's
no place for the Holy Face!" The "Holy Face" refers to an ancient wooden crucifix in Lucca's cathedral. According to legend,
its sculptor fell asleep and, when he awoke, found the statue mi-
raculously completed by Nicodemus, a Pharisee who defended

Christ when the other Pharisees denounced him. Consequently, many Lucchese swear by this crucifix. But the Sacred Face will be of no help to Lucchese barrators in Hell. The devils chortle—in Hell one swims differently than in the Serchio, the river that runs south of Lucca.

We see Dante's comic flair again in his treatment of the Sienese. In *Inferno* 29, Dante has a breezy exchange with the alchemist Griffolino, who confesses that he once duped the son of the bishop of Siena into thinking that he could teach him to fly. The bishop had Griffolino hanged for the deception. Dispensing this time with roundabout allusion, Dante accuses the Sienese of vanity and names some of the city's most frivolous citizens:

> And I said to the poet, "Now was ever a people so vain as the Sienese? Surely not so the French by far."
>
> Whereat the other leper, who heard me, responded to my words, "Except for the Stricca, who knew how to spend in moderation; and except for Niccolò, who first devised the costly use of the clove, in the garden where such seed takes root; and except for the company in which Caccia d'Ascanio squandered the vineyard and Abbagliato showed his wit."
> (*Inf.* 29.121–32)

Here Dante kills two birds with one stone—hitting two of his favorite targets, the Sienese and the French. His list of silly Sienese includes Stricca, Niccolò, Caccia d'Asciano, and Abbagliato. All extravagant profligates, these four men were members of the Brigata Spendereccia (Spendthrift Club), a group of wealthy noblemen of Siena whose members contributed to a lavish fund that they had to spend or risk expulsion from the group. The group squandered all the money in two years by holding extravagant banquets and indulging in trivial pastimes. In line 128, we have an allusion to one of the luxurious practices of the group, Niccolò's use of costly cloves to season food. Caccia d'Asciano and Abbagliato blithely destroyed all the dishes and cutlery after one of their glorious meals. One commentator reports that they spent 216,000 florins in two years, roughly the equivalent of 16 to 19 million dollars in today's terms. Dante is clearly more interested in highlighting the ridiculousness of the Sienese than in pursuing the sins of Griffolino. Like his association of Lucca with barratry, Dante relishes linking Siena (and the French) with frivolity. There is comedy in the *Comedy!*

## THE RUIN OF PUBLIC SPACE: GARDINGO

At such moments, characters seem to draw conclusions about Lucca and Siena based on the evidence of damned souls. A familiar stereotype about the town finds confirmation in Dante's visit to the underworld. One can imagine that the poet might have depicted Cahors, earlier used as a coded reference to usury, with the comic or judgmental amplification he applies to Lucca or to Siena. Here the trip to Hell clarifies and confirms, with a kind of finality, an earthly sentiment.

At other moments, Dante goes beyond this distinctive use of place. Instead of confirming stereotypes, he maps Italy in a more pointed way, by focusing on some of the country's most notorious crime scenes. It is as if he has created a special overlay, one that shines a spotlight on the sites of the foulest crimes of his times. One might see this as the poet's effort to map an infernal world on Earth.

During Dante's encounter with the hypocrites Catalano and Loderingo in *Inferno* 23, the former acknowledges:

> We were Jovial Friars, and Bolognese: I named Catalano,
> and he Loderingo, and by your city chosen together, as one
> man alone is usually chosen, to maintain the peace; and we

were such, that it still appears around the Gardingo. (*Inf.*
23.103–108)

Few references in the *Inferno* are as local as this. Among Dante's
first readers, likely only Tuscans recognized the significance of
the reference to Gardingo. Originally the name for a defensive
tower, Gardingo was the area in which the Uberti, the heads of
the Ghibelline party in Florence, had their palaces. Today this is
the site of the Palazzo Vecchio. As we noted in the last chapter,
the two Friars did not act even-handedly, allowing the destruction of the Uberti palaces. As Catalano admits, the place is tied
intimately to the criminal: "we were such that it still appears
around the Gardinga" (*Inf.* 23.107–8). The blighted site attests
to the hypocrisy and duplicity of the two friars, who sided with
the winning party rather than govern justly.[4]

Just as Hell has an order, in which sins are both punished
and represented by the contrapasso, so do certain notorious
locales achieve the lucidity and justice of divine judgment. As
he descends through Hell, Dante the pilgrim learns to read Hell;
similarly, he begins to ponder Earth's sad history of deceit and
fraud. Dante applies the meticulous structure of Hell, which
carefully separates sins and sorts sinners within an elaborate yet
legible array, to Earth, creating his own parallel structure—a
Hell on Earth. As we shall see later when we examine adaptations and reuses of the *Inferno,* this impulse becomes a powerful technique in modern literature and popular culture. Many
modern authors, following Dante's example, will map Hell
onto their own particular place and time.

## A NOTORIOUS CRIME SCENE:
## THE MEDITERRANEAN

Dante's meeting with the schismatic Pier da Medicina offers another opportunity to associate a place with an infamous crime.

Little is known of this man aside from what is revealed in *Inferno* 28, which informs us that Pier sowed discord between two powerful noble families, the Malatesta and the Polenta, in the Romagna (a region of central Italy). This circle's punishment lies in the action of a devil that literally puts each sinner to the sword. Since Pier fomented division by making inflammatory accusations, the punishment addresses the means of communication directly—the sinner's ears, nose, and windpipe are mutilated. Forced to communicate through his open windpipe, blood spews everywhere each time Pier speaks.

> Another who had his throat pierced through and his nose cut off up to the eyebrows, and only one ear left, stopped with the rest to gaze in astonishment, and before the others opened his gullet, which was all red outside, and said, "O you whom guilt does not condemn and whom I saw above in the land of Italy, if too great likeness does not deceive me, if ever you return to see the sweet plain that slopes from Vercelli to Marcabò, remember Pier da Medicina. And make it known to the two best men of Fano, to messer Guido and to Angiolello, that unless our foresight here is vain, they will be thrown out of their vessel and sunk near La Cattolica, through the treachery of a fell tyrant. Between the islands of Cyprus and Majorca Neptune never saw so great a crime, not of the pirates nor of the Argolic people. That traitor who sees with but one eye, and holds the city from sight of which one who is here with me would wish he had fasted, will make them come to parley with him, then will so deal with them that for the wind of Focara they will not need vow or prayer. (*Inf.* 28.64–90)

Here again, by virtue of the fact that Dante sets his visionary journey in 1300, he puts himself in the position of seeming to predict what has already passed. In line 77, Pier makes a prophecy and tells Dante to warn Guido del Cassero and Angiolello di Carignano that a treacherous one-eyed tyrant (Malatestino da Rimini) will drown them. Guido and Angiolello belonged to opposing factions in Fano, a town in the Marches region of Italy. Pier's prophecy refers to their death by drowning in 1312. Malatestino planned these murders so he could take over the lordship of Fano.

Pier's is the longest speech made by any of the schismatics. The passage is saturated with reference to place—no fewer than eight locales are mentioned. Some of the references—Medicina, Vercelli, and Marcabò—allude to the area from which Pier hails. Medicina is a small town in Emilia and site of a one-time fortress. Vercelli is a town in Piedmont, and Marcabò is the name of a castle in the territory of Ravenna. These places, in Dante's telling, become notorious because of Pier's infamous association with them. Fano is a coveted territory: The tyrant killed two of the city's "best" men in order to increase his territorial holdings. Malatestino invited Guido and Angiolello to a meeting, then ordered them intercepted and drowned while they were at sea. In line 80, the term *"mazzerati,"* translated simply as "sunk" by Singleton, refers to the practice of throwing someone into the sea tied in a sack with a huge stone to weight it down.

Malatestino's treachery exceeds any crime committed in the Mediterranean—from its eastern boundary in Cyprus to its western point in Mallorca. In all his years, Neptune, god of the seas, has never witnessed anything so villainous. Pier da Medicina ironically notes that Guido and Angiolello need not fear being shipwrecked: He knows they'll be drowned off the coast of La Cattolica, a small town on the Adriatic between Rimini and Pesaro. Just as Gardingo attests to the hypocrisy of Catalano and Loderingo, the Mediterranean bears witness to Malatestino's brutal treachery. The difference is one of scale. In this vast expanse of space and time, no crime committed in the Mediterranean surpasses the brutality of this murder.

The use of place is quite artful here. Pier begins by specify-
ing a range of ground, the "gentle" plain between Vercelli and
Marcabò, and follows this pastoral landscape with a far wider
range of sea, from Cyprus and Majorca, or, more simply, the
reach of the Mediterranean Sea. He essentially specifies a notorious crime scene.

## MEMORY AS PUNISHMENT: ROMENA

Dante's encounter with the counterfeiter Master Adam offers
another fascinating example of the poet's ingenious treatment
of crime sites. We find Master Adam among the other falsifiers.
There are four groups in all, and a different disease afflicts each
group. Falsifiers of metals, or alchemists, suffer from leprosy;
falsifiers of people, or impersonators, from hydrophobia; falsifiers of money, or counterfeiters, from dropsy; and falsifiers of
words, or liars, from a raging fever. Dante's objection to the falsifiers' behavior seems connected to his condemnation of fraud
in general. Perversion of metals, words, currency, and persons
toward deceitful ends is an offense against central principles of
divine order and justice. Falsifiers transform the appearance of
things (people, words, money) and make trust among people
impossible. As such, they strike at the heart of Dante's vision of
a just society by forcing dealings to take place in an atmosphere
of doubt and suspicion. The various diseases stand as an image
of the corruptions that the falsifiers engendered, during their
lives, in the community.

Master Adam recalls his former activities in unusually vivid
terms:

> "Oh you who are without any punishment, and I know
> not why, in this dismal world," he said to us, "behold and
> consider the misery of Master Adam. Living, I had in plenty
> all that I wished, and now, alas! I crave one drop of water!
> The little brooks that from the green hills of Casentino run

down into the Arno, making their channels cool and moist, are always before me, and not in vain, for the image of them parches me far more than the malady that wastes my features. The rigid justice that scourges me draws occasion from the place where I sinned, to give my sighs a quicker flight; there is Romena, where I falsified the currency stamped with the Baptist, for which on earth I left my body burnt." (*Inf.* 30.58–75)

Few recollections are as anguished as Master Adam's. Dante's artistry here is exquisite. First, he reduces Master Adam's suffering to one powerful detail: "I crave one drop of water!" Then he deftly expands that image, moving from droplet to rivulet to the Arno. Similarly, the counterfeiter widens his contemplation from a single drop to various channels of water with different temperatures. God's judgment obliges Master Adam to dwell constantly on the image of the cool stream as an oasis, which coincidentally is also the site of his counterfeiting. In addition to the stream, Master Adam recalls the site of his counterfeiting activity—the castle of Romena. The site of his criminal activity and his punishment are forever intertwined.

As Master Adam explains, he counterfeited the florin, Florence's gold coin. Minted in 1252, the coin was stamped on one side with a lily and with an image of the city's patron, John the Baptist, on the other. Later in the canto he confesses to adding three carats of dross (worthless metal) to his florins. Again Dante draws attention to the negative effects of wealth in Florence, a place that had become a kind of republic of money. Master Adam's counterfeits, undertaken in the new world of quickened commercial activity that Dante decried earlier in the poem, stand in sharp contrast to the natural beauty of the Casentino. The depth of Master Adam's fraud is made manifest by the fact that he corrupts the coin bearing the image of

Florence's patron saint. The need for ever more cash is inextricably tied to increasing commercial interests, the "sudden gains" decried by the three Florentine sodomites in *Inferno* 16, which in turn leads to moral decay. Usury and counterfeiting follow almost as a matter of course.

## THE HUNGER TOWER

Master Adam is not the only soul in Hell to recall with great pain the site of his undoing. Ugolino, one of the most memorable of Dante's characters, relays the most gruesome story of death in the entire *Inferno*. The pilgrim first comes across Ugolino while making his way across Antenora, the area of Cocytus reserved for traitors to homeland or party. Only the heads of these traitors, who are immersed in the ice, are visible. The sight of two sinners, one gnawing on the brains of the other, arrests the pilgrim's attention. Dante compares this grisly spectacle to a classical instance of hatred from Statius's *Thebaid*, in which Tydeus, mortally wounded, manages nevertheless to kill his assailant, Menalippus, by chewing on his head. This chilling scene of cannibalism introduces us to one of Dante's most shocking treatments of place.

The feeding soul, who speaks to Dante after wiping his lips on his victim's hair, is Count Ugolino della Gherardesca; the other is Ruggieri, archbishop of Pisa from 1278 to 1295. Dante condemns both as traitors to their political parties. Count Ugolino was a member of one of the most prominent Ghibelline families of Pisa. In 1275 (after the Guelf triumph at Benevento, which inaugurated Guelf domination of Tuscany), Ugolino switched his loyalties to the Guelf party. After conspiring with one of the Guelf leaders to seize control of Pisa, traditionally a Ghibelline city, he was banished.

Despite much opposition, Ugolino managed to return to Pisa within a year and to engineer his election as *podesta*, a mayor-like position. Pisa's situation at this time was very precarious since other Tuscan cities—Florence, Genoa, and Lucca—were forming an alliance against it. In 1285, Ugolino ceded some of Pisa's castles to Florence, which enraged many Pisans and exacerbated party divisions. Subsequently, Ugolino aligned himself more closely with the Ghibellines, headed by Archbishop Ruggieri and supported by powerful Pisan families, such as the Lanfranchi, Gualandi, and Sismondi. Ultimately, the traitor was himself betrayed. The archbishop, notorious for his double dealing, incited public opinion against Ugolino and condemned him for having ceded Pisa's castles. Under the guise of negotiating a new agreement, the archbishop summoned Ugolino to Pisa, imprisoned him along with two sons and two grandsons, and saw that the five starved to death in captivity.

The story of Ugolino's imprisonment and death was familiar to all Tuscans. Upon seeing Dante, the count seizes the opportunity to relay what was less well known, namely the gruesome manner of his death and that of his children and grandchildren. As he begins his story, he transports us immediately to the scene of the family's imprisonment.

> You have to know that I was Count Ugolino, and this is the Archbishop Ruggieri. Now I will tell you why I am such a neighbor to him. How, by effect of his ill devising, I, trusting in him, was taken and thereafter put to death, there is no need to tell; but what you cannot have heard, that is, how cruel my death was, you shall hear and you shall know if he has wronged me.
>
> A narrow hole in the Mew which because of me has the title of Hunger, and in which others are yet to be shut up, had, through its opening, already shown me several moons, when I had the bad dream that rent for me the veil of the future. (*Inf.* 33.22–27)

The prison looms large in Ugolino's sorrowful account. The smallness of its one window underscores the men's extreme confinement. In these lines, Ugolino refers to the prison variously as the Mew and the Hunger Tower. Elsewhere in the canto he describes it as "horrible" and "woeful." The tower of the Gualandi family served as a prison through 1318. It was also known as the Eagles' Tower because the Pisan commune kept its eagles there during their nesting periods. Significantly, Ugolino renames it, giving it the "title of Hunger" because of the cruel way in which he and his family were put to death. (Dante heightens the pathos of the situation by changing details of the story. Two of the victims were Ugolino's grandsons, and three of the four "sons" were adults. Yet Dante presents them all as Ugolino's vulnerable children.)

Gazing out the window, Ugolino marks the passage of the days and months. In line 26, he recalls a terrifying dream portraying a violent hunt in which a man tracks a wolf and its whelps until they are caught and dismembered by voracious hounds. Ugolino identifies the hounds as the Gualandi, Sismondi, and Lanfranchi, the Pisan families that assisted the vindictive archbishop Ruggieri in hunting down the wolf and his whelps, clearly Ugolino and his sons.

Upon awakening, Ugolino sees his hungry sons expecting their customary meal to be brought to them. Instead, they hear the door of the prison being nailed shut. He relays horrible scenes of anguish between himself and his sons, as each day of suffering brings with it new grief. Over the course of a week, the four sons die of starvation, beginning with Gaddo's death on the fourth day, followed by the other three on the fifth and sixth days. Severely weakened and blind, Ugolino crawls about calling out after his dead children. Just before his own death, he declares "fasting did more than grief had done" (line 75). With this enigmatic remark, Ugolino returns to the archbishop's skull and continues his macabre feast of retribution.

Monstrous as this story is, many readers have found even more appalling implications to his final words. Since the Renaissance, commentators to the poem have debated the ambiguity of Ugolino's final remark. Is what is unspoken here the unspeakable act of cannibalism, or simply a speechless death by starvation? The syntax of the original Italian permits either reading, although the majority of commentators opt for the less repellent alternative.

Outraged over the persecution of Ugolino's innocent children, Dante launches into a fierce attack on Pisa in line 89.

Ah, Pisa! shame of the peoples of the fair land where the *sì* is heard, since your neighbors are slow to punish you, let Capraia and Gorgona shift, and make a hedge for Arno at its mouth, so that it drown every soul in you! For if Count Ugolino had the name of betraying you of your castles, you ought not to have put his children to such torture. Their youthful years, you modern Thebes, made Uguiccione and Brigata innocent, and the other two that my song names above. (*Inf.* 33.79–90)

Such an excess of evil renews the horrors of Thebes, another cursed city. Sown from dragon's teeth, Thebes was notorious in myth for parricide, fratricide, and incest. Oedipus became King of Thebes after he killed his father, Laius, whom he did not recognize. He then—also unwittingly—married his mother. Finally, his two sons, Eteocles and Polynices, killed one another. In his outrage with the savage retribution of the Pisans, Dante wishes that Caprara and Gorgona, two islands northeast of Corsica, which belonged to Pisa, might block the mouth of the Arno so that all Pisans would be drowned. This new Thebes deserves complete annihilation.

There is no lack of intensity in Dante's excoriation and damnation of sinners, places, and cities in the *Divine Comedy,* but this treatment of Pisa is especially severe—even apocalyptic in its imagined destruction. If we read closely, Dante's fulmination seems strangely contradictory: He damns an entire city, which would presumably contain both the innocent and the guilty, partly for the crime of executing innocent children—in other words, for indiscriminate killing. Although he registers disgust and horror at the excessive nature of the archbishop's punishment, Dante responds with even more excess.

This passage, coming near the end of the *Inferno,* is a culmination of both the horror and the artistry of the poem. What Dante the pilgrim sees before him is certainly one of Eliot's "clear visual images"—one man gnawing the brains of another—but equally memorable is the detail of Ugolino's account: the daybreak, which slowly reveals the faces of the count's hungry children; the sound of the door of the tower being nailed shut; Ugolino's savage biting of his own hands; and finally, darkness, as the blind count passes his hands over the corpses of his sons.

Shakespeare, in one of his most memorable passages, allows one of his characters to comment on the poet's art:

> The poet's eye, in a fine frenzy rolling,
> Doth glance from heaven to earth, from earth to heaven;
> And as imagination bodies forth
> The forms of things unknown, the poet's pen
> Turns them to shapes, and gives to aery nothing
> A local habitation and a name. (*A Midsummer Night's Dream,*
>    5.1.12–7)

This might well describe Dante's achievement. His poem deals with "things unknown"—the infernal, purgatorial, and heavenly realms—but it also locates and names things on this Earth. Thirst, for Master Adam, is less an abstraction than the creation of an intricate concatenation of lovely watery forms.

Abstract terms like "hunger" and "starvation" in Ugolino's account become a harrowing list of moving details. But in each case, the total effect bends to a renaming of place, whether Master Adam's green hills of the Casentino or a well-known civic building.

In a larger sense, Dante charts two realms in the poem. His stated aim in the *Divine Comedy* is to record his vision of the afterlife, but that record involves intricate recollections and descriptions of the human world. Ultimately, his account of the world is less a contrast to than a dismaying extension of the Hell he depicts. Hell abides both in the afterlife and on Earth. Mapping Hell initiates an infernal map of human corruption. Dante's conception is very close to more modern ones of damnation—Hell is as much a spiritual condition as a physical space of bodily punishment.

# 6

# The Legacy of Dante's Inferno

We've been exploring Dante's world and aspects of the *Inferno* that lend themselves to adaptation and reuse—how the choices Dante made as he wrote his poem created opportunities for later writers. Now let's see what writers have made of this legacy. In this chapter, we'll look at how writers who operate in high culture have exploited Dante; in the next chapter, we'll examine more popular versions and appropriations of the poem. We'll have a few more things to say about this distinction between high and low culture as well.

This chapter isn't meant to be an exhaustive treatment of Dante's legacy. In fact, we'll stick to examples from the English-speaking tradition, despite the importance of the *Divine Comedy* throughout Europe and the Americas. We want to show how Dante's work has spurred the imagination of subsequent writers, and that is best done by tracing a sequence of works.

## AN INFERNO OF THE MIND:
## JOHN MILTON'S *PARADISE LOST*

John Milton's *Paradise Lost* is an obvious place to begin this discussion. Milton's epic poem, which seeks, as the poet puts it, to "justify the ways of God to men" by retelling the story of the fall put forth in the Old Testament, recalls and reworks the *Inferno* in many ways. Milton's boldest revision of the Dantesque tradition lies in his presentation of Satan. In Dante's poem, Satan is monumental. Huge, immobile, and terrifying, he is the culminating spectacle of the infernal journey:

> If he was once as beautiful as he is ugly now, and lifted up his brows against his Maker, well may all sorrow proceed from him. Oh how great a marvel it was to me when I saw three faces on his head: one in front and it was red, and the other two joined to this just over the middle of each shoulder, and all were joined at the crown. The right one seemed between white and yellow, and the left one was such in appearance as are those who come from whence the Nile descends. From under each there came forth two mighty wings, of size befitting such a bird—sails at sea I never saw so broad. They had no feathers, but were like a bat's. And he was flapping them, so that three winds went forth from him, whereby Cocytus was all congealed. (*Inf.* 34. 34–52)

Dante's Satan is more an object than a character. In fact, so tightly is he fitted to the infernal schemes of punishment that he seems a part of Hell's infrastructure. His wings cool the lowest regions of Hell to freezing, effectively providing the medium of suffering for those traitors encased in ice. And he slowly chews three arch-sinners: Judas, Cassius, and Brutus. He is a terrifying figure but an oddly removed presence. He takes no notice of Dante or Virgil as they scurry beneath him, climb down his body, and pass on to the happier region of Purgatory.

To see some of what Milton learned from Dante's example, we need only look at one of the first speeches from Book I of *Paradise Lost,* in which Satan, having been defeated by God and his faithful angels, has just raised himself from a lake of fire in which he and the other rebel angels have been lying helpless and dazed:

> "Is this the region, this the soil, the clime,"
> Said then this lost Archangel, "this the seat
> That we must change for Heaven, this mournful gloom
> For that celestial light? Be it so, since he
> Who now is sovereign can dispose and bid
> What shall be right. Farthest from him is best
> Whom reason hath equaled, force hath made supreme
> Above his equals." (*Par. Lost* 1.242–249)

This mixture of grandeur and low cunning recalls the complex psychologies of many of the damned souls in the *Inferno*. Satan shows implacable resistance to overwhelming force, which we cannot help but admire, but he also reveals his ethical limitations, as he asserts that God's "right" is simply a manifestation of his power, not some display of justice. Satan persists in his original error of pride, insisting on his equality with God in reason and arguing that God's superior force is simply an accident. We need only to glance at some of Dante's most famous set speeches in the *Inferno*, such as Farinata's arrogant fulminations on Tuscan politics in canto 10 or Ugolino's tormented memories of his imprisonment in canto 33, to see how Milton channeled Dante's unusual combination of great dramatic immediacy and remarkable concision into this character. We might also note how Milton extends Dante's practice. Dante's concision—the brevity of even the speeches of the damned—becomes, in Milton's hands, density. Satan's speeches are longer, but he maintains the weight of Dante's expression.

The psychological contradictions and evasions so prominent in this passage from Milton continue throughout Satan's speeches. Like many of the damned in Dante's poem, Milton's Satan gives an eloquent and intricate account of himself—one that mingles heroism and corruption and mixes powerful rhetoric and self-serving, evasive language. "Here, at least," he boasts, "we shall be free" (*Par. Lost* 1.258), cleverly redefining freedom entirely. "Better to reign in Hell than serve in Heaven" (*Par. Lost* 1.263), he quips, putting the best face on the catastrophic defeat he has led his "associates and copartners" into. Satan's most moving assertions are at the same time subtle rationalizations, exercises in evading responsibility and shirking blame. Like many of Dante's damned souls, Milton's Satan is a study in exquisite ironies. Milton has clearly learned much from Dante's compressed and suggestive rhetoric.

Hell, for Milton, is a place of intense physical torment and torture. His description of the "burning marl," as he terms it, is very palpable, very tangible; one feels the fire and smells the smoke of combustion. In that, Milton's Hell is like Dante's. But as Satan speaks, his emphasis is not so much on his physical circumstances as on the power of the mind to transform them:

> Receive thy new possessor: one who brings
> A mind not to be changed by place or time.
> The mind is its own place, and in itself
> Can make a Heaven of Hell, a Hell of Heaven. (*Par. Lost*
> 1.252–255)

One might say that as Satan lifts himself out of the burning lake, he also raises himself from the torments of Dante's intensely physical vision of Hell in the *Inferno* to a psychological conception of damnation, one more in line with Renaissance ideas of the primacy of the mind. We can see this later in the poem, when Satan gives a tormented account of his situation:

> Me miserable! Which way shall I fly
> Infinite wrath, and infinite despair?
> Which way I fly is Hell: myself am Hell;
> And in the lowest deep a lower deep
> Still threatening to devour me opens wide,
> To which the Hell I suffer seems a Heaven. (*Par. Lost*
>     4.73–78)

Milton keeps much of Dante in his account of Hell in *Paradise Lost,* but he adds something else: the sense of Hell being not so much a place, a material world, but a state of mind. In a sense, what is most characteristically medieval about Dante's conception of Hell—its physicality—is updated by Milton, the most characteristic of Renaissance thinkers.

## COMPETITION AND RESPECT: TWO NINE-TEENTH-CENTURY USES OF DANTE

Sometimes poets recall Dante not to contest or emend but to honor him. Such is the case with the 1842 poem "Ulysses" by Alfred, Lord Tennyson. In the compactness of its presentation, the expanse of its rhetoric, the subtlety of characterization of its speaker, and the beauty of its language, Tennyson's portrayal rivals Dante's portrait of this mythological figure in *Inferno* 26. Tennyson seems most struck by the power of persuasive speech and noble view of the purpose of life of Dante's Ulysses, and his poem has an exuberance that recalls Dante's famous lines: "Consider your origin: you were not made to live as brutes, but to pursue virtue and knowledge" (*Inf.* 26. 118–120). No one could read Tennyson's poem and not be moved by the speaker's exhortation to "Follow knowledge, like a sinking star, / Beyond the utmost bound of human thought" (31–2).

But however respectful of Dante's poem Tennyson might be, he nevertheless transforms Ulysses' message in an interesting way. Dante puts Ulysses' profound desire to explore and to seek into a Christian framework, one that suggests that such activity is ultimately foolish or vain. Ulysses' speech in the *Inferno* ends in death, as his ship, sailing beyond the limits of the known world, nears an ominous dark mountain (possibly Purgatory) and founders in a whirlwind. Ulysses registers, albeit obliquely, the retributive nature of this catastrophe with the aside "as pleased Another" (*Inf.* 26.141). Tennyson also contextualizes Ulysses' desire. A good Victorian, he compares Ulysses' explorations and search for "new things" to the more sober and prudent work of his son, Telemachus, who endeavors to govern well, to civilize his people, and to make them "useful and good." Tennyson puts Ulysses' voyage in social terms, contrasting the son's communal efforts with his father's irresponsible wandering. Each poet undermines his eloquent and seductive speaker with another view of his activity, and each implicit criticism tells us much about the deeper commitments of the age: Dante to Christian faith and Tennyson to the gospel of social improvement. Ulysses' voyage, in each poem, is foolish and leads to death. But Tennyson redistributes the tension in Dante's presentation, and in doing so he is able to suit Ulysses' story to his particular historical moment.

Such solemn respect is not always accorded Dante's poem. John Keats, in his 1821 poem "Lamia," recalls the *Inferno* with an attitude of friendly competition. His poem's femme fatale, the title's Lamia, begins the story as a snake. Keats records her transformation from serpent to beautiful woman with gusto. He brilliantly recalls Dante's description in *Inferno* 24 and 25 of the thieves, whose punishment for theft is to have their own bodies stolen. Dante exults in his poetic skill as he narrates the process, in which a serpent attacks a thief, fuses with him, and then exchanges his snaky features for human form. Noting that earlier poets—particularly Lucan and Ovid—had described such metamorphoses, Dante insists on his triumph over his poetic forebears. He taunts Ovid: "I envy him not; for two natures front to front he never so transmuted that both forms were prompt to exchange their substance" (*Inf.* 25.100–102). Dante then launches into a virtuoso description of the transformation, one that might well justify his insolence.

Keats, as the moment of metamorphosis approaches in his own poem, knows full well that some of his readers would recall this passage from Dante. He does not boast of his creative prowess, as Dante does, but he does his best to outdo Dante in this contest of transformations:

Left to herself, the serpent now began
To change; her elfin blood in madness ran,
Her mouth foam'd, and the grass, therewith besprent,
Wither'd at dew so sweet and virulent;
Her eyes in torture fix'd, and anguish drear,
Hot, glaz'd, and wide, with lid-lashes all sear,
Flash'd phosphor and sharp sparks, without one cooling tear.
The colours all inflam'd throughout her train,
She writh'd about, convuls'd with scarlet pain:
A deep volcanian yellow took the place
Of all her milder-mooned body's grace;
And, as the lava ravishes the mead,
Spoilt all her silver mail, and golden brede;
Made gloom of all her frecklings, streaks and bars,
Eclips'd her crescents, and lick'd up her stars:
So that, in moments few, she was undrest
Of all her sapphires, greens, and amethyst,
And rubious-argent: of all these bereft,
Nothing but pain and ugliness were left.

Still shone her crown; that vanish'd, also she
Melted and disappear'd as suddenly . . . ("Lamia" 1.146–166)

No vaunting here, no braggadocio, but Keats pivots from
Dante's flashy display of poetic technique to his own bit of exuberant revelry in description. Keats is reverential to his source,
but he seems to relish the friendly competition that such a passage initiates. One might, in fact, argue that Keats's decision to
compete with Dante is, in itself, the greatest tribute to the poet.
Keats follows the lesson of Dante's ambition and applies it to
his illustrious forebear's own poem.

## HELL ON EARTH:
## DANTE AND LITERARY MODERNISM

Perhaps no literary movement in the British and American tradition turned to Dante as resolutely as modernism. Two poets
who figure prominently in this movement, T. S. Eliot and Ezra
Pound, looked to Dante for some of their most profound inspi-
rations. Literary modernism is a complex movement, but on
one level it is a reaction to some of the great insights of the
nineteenth century: to Karl Marx, whose theories trace consciousness to the economic basis of life; to Friedrich Nietzsche,
who insists that human consciousness is merely an evolutionary
state and might well pass away; and to Sigmund Freud, whose
theory of unconscious drives suggests that our everyday idea
of consciousness is at best incomplete and possibly an illusion.
The result of this intellectual foment was a widely held feel-
ing among artists and intellectuals at the time that traditional
values, as Nietzsche put it, had to be reformulated. They could
not come, as they had in Dante's, Milton's, or even Tennyson's
time, from a god in heaven. Some thinkers felt exhilarated by
the freedom offered by such a reassessment; others felt a deep

sense of loss and often a sense of revulsion toward what they see as the meaningless and arbitrary world about them.

As a literary movement, Modernism was in part a reaction against the realistic narratives of the past century. Modernist writers preferred what they called a "mythic" method, in which their narratives would, through consistent reference to myth, undermine their surface realism. An example of this is James Joyce's *Ulysses,* a novel which primarily traces, in unflinching detail, a day in the life of two twentieth century Dubliners, but which parallels their activities and moods to episodes from Homer's *Odyssey.*

We can see this kind of intricate counterpoint of psychological realism and mythic structure in one of T. S. Eliot's most famous poems, "The Love Song of J. Alfred Prufrock" (1915). On one level, the poem is a transcript of the speaker's innermost thoughts and anxieties about his futile, barren life in a squalid city. Prufrock is intensely self-conscious, relentlessly intellectual, and profoundly unable to commit himself to any course of action. But Eliot is not satisfied with this straightforwardly realistic presentation. He makes this clear at once by quoting part of Guido da Montefeltro's speech in *Inferno* 27 as an epigraph to the poem:

> If I thought that my answer were to one who might ever return to the world, this flame would shake no more; but since from this depth none ever returned alive, if what I hear is true, I answer you without fear of infamy. (*Inf.* 27.61–6)

(Eliot quotes the Italian; we provide a translation.) Through this flashy reference, Eliot urges us to read Prufrock's confession as that of a damned soul in Hell, one who suffers and speaks but who mistakenly thinks his words will not be carried back to the world of the living. The connection between Prufrock and

Guido emphasizes the depth of repression involved in everyday life for Eliot, as well as his sense that many of the rootless urbanites in his poems were, in a sense, dead. Prufrock's indecision and sense of futility mark his confession:

> There will be time, there will be time
> To prepare a face to meet the faces that you meet;
> . . . . . . . . . . . . . . . . . . . . . . . . . . . . . . . . . . . . .
> Time for you and time for me,
> And time yet for a hundred indecisions,
> And for a hundred visions and revisions,
> Before the taking of toast and tea. ("Prufrock" 26–7, 32–4)

The implication here is that modern urban life is a kind of Hell, in which city dwellers are damned to punishments no less various and horrible than those described in Dante. Eliot takes Milton's psychological conception of Hell, in which Hell is not so much a place as a condition, and applies it to a world that repels him. But behind this act of homage to Milton lies a more profound homage to Dante.

This mythic technique is exploited even more brilliantly in Eliot's 1922 "Waste Land," another of modernism's signature pieces. The first section of this difficult poem combines allusions to past literary masterpieces and rapidly sketched vignettes to present a chaotic, meaningless world in which damned souls register their suffering. "Prufrock" is framed as a kind of evening stroll, in which the speaker begins by courteously enjoining the reader ("Let us go then, you and I") to take in the sights and sounds of the city. Eliot's "Waste Land" adopts this rambling structure as well, in which readers "visit," as Prufrock puts it, this urban netherworld. In a particularly brilliant use of this technique, Eliot describes part of the morning commute to work in London:

> Unreal city,
> Under the brown fog of a winter dawn,
> A crowd flowed over London Bridge, so many,
> I had not thought death had undone so many.
> Sighs, short and infrequent, were exhaled,
> And each man fixed his eyes before his feet. ("Waste Land"
>    60–66)

The fourth line is a literal translation of *Inferno* 3.55–57, in which Dante the pilgrim describes the souls in Limbo, and the next line recalls descriptions in the next canto. The suggestion here is that Hell is now on Earth; that London is Dis, the infernal city; that modern life is a kind of damnation. In one brilliant stroke of allusion, Eliot expresses his deep horror at the anomie, rootlessness, and lack of conviction typical of modern life.

Eliot keeps up this insistent parallel of the modern city with Dante's *Inferno* throughout the poem. The glimpses we get of modern life, such as those in the second section of the poem, which concern relations between men and women, show a profound alienation. We overhear a terrible conversation between a woman who borders on hysteria and a cruelly unresponsive man. As she becomes urgent, he settles into a morbid despondency:

> The hot water at ten
> And if it rains, the closed car at four.
> And we shall play a game of chess,
> Pressing lidless eyes and waiting for a knock upon the door.
>    ("Waste Land" 135–138)

Like so many of the characters in Eliot's poem, the man can look forward only to an eternity of routine, boredom, and pointlessness—a spiritless death in life.

The section concludes with a ghastly conversation in a pub near closing time, where two women, an unnamed speaker and Lil, discuss the demobilization of Lil's husband. A hero returning from World War I, Albert expects "a good time," and he also expects Lil to have smartened up a bit in his absence:

> He'll want to know what you done with that money he gave
>     you
> To get yourself some teeth. He did, I was there,
> You have them all out, Lil, and get a nice set,
> He said, I swear, I can't bear to look at you. ("Waste Land"
>     142–146)

Lil attributes her decline in looks to an abortion (another of the poem's recurrent failures of fertility), and the speaker insinuates that Albert might find his welcome with her, if Lil insists on looking "so antique." The thoughtless amorality of this episode concludes with a nice Sunday dinner, "a hot gammon," with the speaker recalling "the beauty of it." The lovelessness, decay, cynicism, hopelessness, and confusion of purpose of the characters are on full display during this "visit."

Eliot draws freely on the *Inferno* throughout his poem, but perhaps no more brilliantly than when he presents Tiresias, a classical figure who was a prophet, wandering amid the everyday people and events of London. His account of a sexual encounter between a bored typist and an opportunistic clerk has all the precision of Dante's sharply focused encounters:

> The time is now propitious, as he guesses,
> The meal is ended, she is bored and tired,
> Endeavours to engage her in caresses
> Which still are unreproved, if undesired. ("Waste Land"
>     235–238)

Her indifference is enough for him; no participation on her part is necessary. Concise yet resonant, the passage demonstrates the meaninglessness of modern life, in which even the most intimate encounters are empty, and where desire has become mechanical.

Eliot's use of Dante's *Inferno* tends to be conceptual. His friend and fellow poet Ezra Pound took a more technical approach in his appropriation of Dante. In his epic poem, *The Cantos,* written over many years, Pound performs a kind of ventriloquism in which he employs Dante's savage indignation to express his dissatisfaction with modernity. In canto 14, Pound constructs his own Hell to punish a variety of modern sins, such as political demagoguery, war profiteering, financial chicane, and corruption of language. His training as a student of Romance languages at the University of Pennsylvania had given Pound a very precise sense of the range of poetic language that Dante employed in his poem, and here Pound recalls Dante's coarser, blunter word choice:

> Io venni in luogo d'ogni luce muto;
> > The stench of wet coal, politicians
> > . . . . . . e and . . . . n, their wrists bound to their ankles,
> > Standing bare bum,
> > Faces smeared on their rumps,
> > > wide eye on flat buttock,
> > Bush hanging for beard,
> > > Addressing crowds through their arse-holes,
> > Addressing the multitudes in the ooze,
> > . . . . . . . . . . . . . . . . . . . . . . . . . . . . . . . . . .
> > Profiteers drinking blood sweetened with shit,
> > And behind them. . . . . . f and the financiers
> > > lashing them with steel wires. (*The Cantos,* XIV.1–10,
> 21–3)

Pound, like Eliot, formally signals his debt to Dante. He begins with a quotation from *Inferno 5*, which quickly alerts the reader to the infernal landscape to come, and then he launches into a disgustingly precise description of sins and the fitness of their punishments. Politicians—clearly demagogues—address crowds through their "arse-holes"; profiteers drink blood sweetened with shit. Later he attacks hypocritical moral reformers—"vice-crusaders, farting through silks." We might recall Dante's description of flatterers in *Inferno* 18, who are punished by being immersed in excrement, or the exuberant profanity of the demon Barbariccia: "And he made a trumpet of his arse" (*Inf.* 21.139).

Pound has learned his Dante lesson well, employing a direct, elemental diction with shocking effect. He ends this particular section of his poem by projecting moral failure onto the landscape, fusing the two much as Dante does in sections of his poem:

> The slough of unamiable liars,
>     bog of stupidities,
> malevolent stupidities, and stupidities,
> the soil living pus, full of vermin,
> dead maggots begetting live maggots,
>     slum owners,
> usurers squeezing crab lice, pandars to authority . . . (*The Cantos*, XIV.68–74)

Just as Dante's *Inferno* reflects the sins of the damned it contains, so does Pound's Hell on earth reflect the transgressions of its inmates.

We wish to conclude with one of the most effective Dantesque passages in modernist poetry, which occurs in T. S. Eliot's "Little Gidding." This is the last in a series of poems called *Four Quartets* in which Eliot explores the place of religion in modern society in a way that recalls Dante the pilgrim's struggles with his faith. In his search for religious fulfillment in what seemed to him a godless, chaotic world, Eliot returned again and again to the figure of Dante, both poet and pilgrim.

In lines 80 to 151 of "Little Gidding," Eliot's speaker walks the streets after an air raid. This undoubtedly has some autobiographical force: Eliot served as a volunteer patrolling the streets of London during the German attacks of World War II. The poem mentions a "dark dove with the flickering tongue"— surely a German plane—and the speaker seems to be moving through the smoldering ruins of a bombed city. This section is written in a modified version of the meter Dante uses in the *Inferno,* terza rima. This is an unusual form for a poet writing in English (it requires far too many rhyme words), and, even in itself, especially in the hands of such an allusive poet as Eliot, the form invokes Dante. But even more Dantesque is the conversation that Eliot's speaker has with what he calls in line 95 his "familiar compound ghost":

> I caught the sudden look of some dead master
> Whom I had known, forgotten, half recalled
> Both one and many; in the brown, baked features
> The eyes of a familiar compound ghost
> Both intimate and unidentifiable.
> So I assumed a double part, and cried
> And heard another's voice cry: "What! are *you* here?" ("Little
> Gidding" 91–100)

The specific reference to the *Inferno* does not come at once in the passage, but it becomes clear through successive hints and allusions. The difficulties in recognition in the light of dusk, the "pointed scrutiny," the "brown, baked features," and the final "What! are *you* here?" all point to the Brunetto Latini episode in *Inferno* 15. What we have here in Eliot's poem is a meeting between the poet/speaker and some past poetic master, a meeting Eliot formally parallels with Dante's encounter with Brunetto. Eliot himself, when asked about the identity of the "familiar compound ghost," mentioned several possible poets, among them William Butler Yeats and Jonathan Swift. Like many remarks by modern poets on their work, that probably isn't all that should be said on the subject. Given Eliot's reliance on Dante, however, such reticence about naming a person should not surprise us. We have noted that Dante's poem, by its very nature, generates mysteries and puzzles of reference. The teasing imprecision of Eliot's "familiar compound ghost" recalls many references to local personages in Dante.

Once we catch the allusion to Dante, other parallels between the two poems present themselves. When speaking of the ingratitude of their contemporaries, Eliot's ghost, like Dante's former teacher Brunetto, adopts a lively vernacular. Brunetto consoles Dante for the envy his fellow Florentines show him: " . . . among the bitter sorb-trees it is not fitting that the sweet fig should come to fruit" (*Inf.* 15.65–66). And Eliot's ghostly interlocutor consoles Eliot for the rapid changes in taste displayed by modern audiences: "For last year's words belong to last year's language / And next year's words await another voice" ("Little Gidding" 120–1). Both ghosts concern themselves with an almost ritual cleansing. Brunetto disparages the Florentines who came from Fiesole, a nearby town: "Old report in the world calls them blind; it is a people avaricious, envious and proud: look that you cleanse yourself of their customs." (*Inf.* 15.67–69) Eliot's ghost concerns himself, as modernist writers tend to do, with language:

> Our concern was speech, and speech impelled us
> To purify the dialect of the tribe
> And urge the mind to aftersight and foresight . . . ("Little
>     Gidding" 128–30)

In each case, the purification has to do with each poet's abiding concern: Dante's with the corruption of civic and political life, Eliot's with the corruption of language.

Finally, in each instance, the speaker from the other world has a warning for the living poet. Brunetto Latini predicts Dante's bitter exile, which he attempts to soothe by urging Dante to follow his star and predicting both honor and renown for him. Eliot's visitant, far less sanguine, dwells bitterly on the infirmities and indignities of an ineffectual old age, predicting only regrets and belated recognition of mistakes. This is Eliot at his mythic game again, setting the certainties and consolations of Dante's intensely Christian world against the anxieties and uncertainties of faith in his century. Dante's poem records, triumphantly, the progress of a blessed soul toward salvation; Eliot's poem can only clutch at an uncertain resolution for his religious doubts. For Eliot, Dante's *Divine Comedy* is a part of the mythic past that he can only marvel at—that he can use as a pattern to structure and to complicate his own poem, but that he cannot return to.

These are only a few examples of reuses and reworkings of Dante's poem by subsequent writers. It's almost as if Dante had provided a how-to guide for later poets, who note the serviceability of Dante's techniques—his insistence on the local, his use of formal and popular language, his pairing of dramatic moments with highly compressed speeches, and his willingness to include mysteries within his presentation—and put these lessons to good use in their own work. Dante's poem has proven an expansive model and inspiration for centuries.

# 7

# *Popular Adaptations of the Inferno*

The distance between high cultural and popular adaptations of classic works of art and literature can seem immense—the one so deliberate and serious, and the other so careless, jocular, or transgressive. Think of the famous cartoon parody of the opera *The Barber of Seville*, in which Elmer Fudd's endlessly fruitless hunt for Bugs Bunny is fitted to Rossini's music. All the zaniness of the cartoon series is in evidence. Elmer Fudd, in full hunting regalia, pursues Bugs, who disguises himself as a barber to evade him. Bugs gives Elmer a ridiculous haircut; later, cross-dressed as a femme fatale, the rabbit lures Elmer to the altar after a monumental chase sequence involving escalating barber chairs. It's Rossini's music, in all its splendor, although the lyrics are fitted to the irony of the trickster rabbit. But, as Thomas Pynchon reminds us in his novel *The Crying of Lot 49*, there is "high magic to low puns." Comedy, even farce, needn't stop us from thinking. The cartoon

Rossini doesn't so much ridicule the opera as ridicule pretention about opera. It asks us to remember that Rossini's opera is just as silly, with the amorous count's impersonation of a drunken soldier, the barber Figaro's preposterous machinations, and the supposedly innocent Rosina's surprising expertise in conducting her affairs under her guardian's nose.

The difference between high and low adaptations of Dante might better be expressed by the terms "reverence" and "respect." Although the distinction between these words has subsided over time into rough equivalence, the older meaning is useful. "Reverence" comes from the Latin *revereor,* meaning "to stand in awe." "Respect," derived from the Latin *respicio,* means "to look back at." Both words have a sense of revisiting, or turning back toward, but the regard of "respect" is more open. Eliot, Pound, and Tennyson, as we saw in the previous chapter, have an almost exaggerated sense of reverence for Dante's text—something like Dante the pilgrim's ecstatic greeting of Virgil at the beginning of the poem: "You are my master and my author. You alone are he from whom I took the fair style that has done me honor" (*Inf.* 1. 85–87).

This reverence signifies one attitude to past work. But other relationships to the past can be productive as well. An homage can be less stately and solemn without loss of power, and many popular appropriations of Dante's poem pay another kind of tribute to their "master" and "author." Sometimes a decided swerve from an authority is the best testimony to the power of the older text.

## BLACK HUMOR AND
## INFERNAL TORMENT:
## POPULAR FILM AND DANTE

Tim Burton's 1988 film *Beetlejuice* includes several ingenious takes on the *Inferno.* It is no surprise that Burton, well known

Fig. 5.    Tim Burton, scene from *Beetlejuice*

for a quirky and opportunistic use of raw materials from both high and popular culture, works largely by distortion and parody. The movie's most obvious allusion to the *Inferno* riffs on the general association of Dante with Hell and sin. Beetlejuice (Michael Keaton) has offered his services to the recently dead Maitlands (Geena Davis and Alec Baldwin) as a "bio-exorcist," that is, someone who will rid them of the pesky living who now occupy their home. To protect the Maitlands from Beetlejuice, the caseworker assigned to help them manage their death distracts Beetlejuice from his sales pitch with a garish strip club/whorehouse, an "Inferno Room" capped by flames and advertising "Girls, Girls, Girls" as well as air-conditioning. (See figure 5.) The humor here is broad, as erotic dancers call to Beetlejuice from the balcony and the trappings of Hell become sleazy enticements to sexual activity.

Less obvious is the film's presentation of the afterlife. If Dante imagines a Hell structured according to medieval theology, with meticulous attention to placing sinners and providing precise punishment for particular sins, Burton's film provides an afterlife modeled after the worst aspects of contemporary bureaucracy. *Beetlejuice* presents an eternity in which the dead wait endlessly for harried and dismissive caseworkers to help them with their problems. The offices are cluttered, the waiting rooms blandly familiar, and the advice utterly useless. Burton's films often cast aspersions on unattractive or grotesque aspects of contemporary life, but *Beetlejuice* slyly suggests that we'll all pay for the bureaucratic nightmare in which we are complicit. There is a contrapasso, but in this case it will be an extension of everyday life in the twentieth century. It'll be funny, but the joke will be on us.

David Fincher's 1995 *Se7en* goes far beyond such playful allusiveness. For Burton, Dante enables a marvelously digressive inset—the Dantesque whorehouse—and a more diffuse gag about the bureaucratic quality of the afterlife. Fincher's movie winds elements from the *Inferno* into the plot more deliberately.

*Se7en* announces its debts to Dante fairly directly. Early in the investigation of several grisly murders, Lieutenant William Somerset (Morgan Freeman) recognizes a pattern based on the medieval scheme of seven deadly sins, and he takes to the New York Public Library—in the dimly lit afterhours, for greatest suspense—to read up on the topic. Dante figures prominently in Somerset's research, and as the camera passes over several books, Fincher takes full advantage of the graphic genius of Gustave Doré's illustrations of the *Inferno,* especially the repellant butchery of the schismatics in canto 28. Bits of Dante's poem (from *Inferno* 28 and 29) appear as well, lines largely ripped from context and all containing violent language.

But Dante's work does more in *Se7en* than provide a blueprint for the killer's exotic and horrific executions. It also structures the relation between the lieutenant and his new partner, David Mills (Brad Pitt). Viewers familiar with the *Inferno* would recognize the older, wiser, and sadder Somerset as the Virgil to Mill's brash young Dante. And on each of these levels, *Se7en* goes beyond the source material to add a surprising change. The killer, John Doe (Kevin Spacey), does not simply emulate the *Inferno*'s punishments. No mere copycat, he seems most drawn to the larger concept of contrapasso. Doe inhabits Dante's world from within, imagining new punishments for old sins that seek to instruct as well as shock his audience. Similarly, the story of *Se7en*'s Virgil and Dante takes a sharp turn from the redemptive journey in the *Inferno*.

The opening scenes sketch an infernal city, a Hell on earth of noise, decay, and driving rain. Somerset treats his first case, unrelated to the serial killer, as routine, however horrific for the viewer—just a particularly messy domestic dispute punctuated by a gunshot that sprays blood on the wall. By contrast, the first of John Doe's murders is both gruesome and suggestive. It presents a kind of tableau, a modern equivalent of Doré's drawings. A morbidly obese man, seated at a squalid kitchen table in his underwear, has died face down in a plate of spaghetti. It is, at once, the image of gluttony, encompassing the sin itself, its disgusting consequences, and a punishment. As Somerset looks past the first impression made by the death scene, the staging becomes as meaningful as the message. Doe has forced the victim, hands and feet tied with barbed wire, to eat until he bursts. The killer's punishment, delivered over 12 hours at gunpoint, includes periodic bouts of vomiting, as the victim's stomach and duodenum are stretched and distended. The detail of the crime extends even to the means, as cans of spaghetti sauce are placed artfully, in a colorful array that recalls Andy Warhol's soup cans.

It's worth contrasting this tableau with Dante's infamous glutton Ciacco, whom the pilgrim encounters in *Inferno* 6. The contrapasso is somewhat murky here:

> I am in the third circle of the eternal, accursed, cold and
> heavy rain: its measure and its quality are never new; huge
> hail, foul water, and snow pour down through the murky air;
> the ground that receives it stinks. (*Inf.* 6.7–12)

The sinners are submerged in a filthy muck, harassed by the triple-headed dog Cerberus, who in classical literature guarded the mouth of the underworld. The contrapasso connects gluttony with a loss of individuality and dignity, in which the sinner is transformed into a beast. John Doe does not simply apply Dante's punishments mechanically. Dante's elusive presentation becomes relentlessly literal in *Se7en*, as the killer works out the details of gluttony with the same intensity of detail that he pursues in his diaries. Doe displays a kind of twisted genius as he builds on the lesson of Dante in crafting his own message.

In fact, one might see Doe vying with Dante—inspired by him but at times seeking to outdo him. Doe seeks, as he puts it to Mills and Somerset, "to turn the sin against the sinner." In this, he follows the law of contrapasso. But where Dante shifts from punishment to purification as he moves from the Inferno to Purgatory, Doe sketches a far darker and more cynical vision. Doe's punishment of sloth, like all his murders, is a carefully staged extravaganza. He leaves clues at the previous crime scene that lead the detectives to think that they have located their man. Tension mounts as we learn the killer's backstory: a repressive childhood; drug, armed robbery, and assault convictions; jail time for the attempted rape of a minor. The police arrive with a flurry of activity—a fleet of police cars, a SWAT team—only to find an immobile, waxen victim. Doe, with his usual sense of theater, has identified the sin clearly by scrawling "Sloth" on the wall above the bed.

Yet again Doe swerves from Dante's precedent by providing a far more literal contrapasso. Dante's slothful, whom we encounter in *Purgatory* 18, must run endlessly, shouting encouragements to each other to keep pace. Their lack of zeal on Earth has now become a manic pursuit of virtue as they ascend the slopes of Purgatory. Yet they hope as they suffer, and they count on release from their trials. Doe revises Dante to match the sour disgust of his view of modern life. Rather than purging sloth, he takes a harder line, focusing on punishment. Doe records the suffering of his victim carefully, making photographs to chart the stages of his decline, and he takes great pains to extend his victim's suffering, plying him with antibiotics and drugs to keep him alive to these torments.

*Se7en* echoes Dante's conception of contrapasso but transforms Dante's idea to suit its purposes. Similarly, the film invokes the Virgil/Dante relation in the *Inferno* only to revise it thoroughly. The allusion is loose but pervasive as Somerset leads Mills through the dark world of corruption and criminality. The sequence in which the detectives discover the victim dedicated to lust makes this pattern clear. Following a lead that leads them to a sex shop that specializes in disturbingly violent apparatus, Somerset and Mills descend into a sleazy and repulsive world of garish light and dim corners. Somerset leads the way, assigning Mills an unwelcome secondary status. In this sequence, the pair does more than simply examine the scene constructed by John Doe. Here, as in the *Inferno,* the two interview denizens of this underworld: the remarkably detached owner of the brothel where the crime takes place and the customer Doe forced to mutilate and kill the victim. These interviews—and especially the tormented confessions of the client—recall the agonized stories of the souls the pilgrim and Virgil meet in the *Inferno.*

But *Se7en* raises Dantesque parallels only to change them. For instance, there is a Beatrice figure in the film, Mills's wife, Tracy (Gwyneth Paltrow), whose innocence in the face of the nightmarish city, however troubled, constitutes one of the few positive aspects of the film. Just as Beatrice brought Virgil and Dante together, Tracy organizes a dinner in which Somerset and Mills begin to overcome their antagonism. The child she carries, despite her doubts about raising it in such menacing circumstances, represents an alternative to the world she inhabits. But *Se7en* departs sharply from the journey to Beatrice familiar to Dante's readers as Tracy ultimately becomes one of Doe's victims, albeit not one representing one of the seven deadly sins. Her decapitation triggers the completion of Doe's plan, an extravagant finale in which the killer moves beyond the static setpieces he constructed earlier in the film to a bit of live theater, in which Mills, now the embodiment of wrath, executes Doe, who takes on the role of envy.

Dante's pilgrim is, above all, a spectator. Although occasionally menaced by devils or moved to punish some sinners, he glides through the world of the damned on a preordained path to both salvation and total revelation. Doe both relies on and revises Dante's poem, making *Se7en* a far bleaker account of the human condition. In Dante's poem, paradoxically, the way down is the way up. For Mills, there is no ascent, no departure from the corrupt and corrupting city. Unlike the promise implicit in the lovely final lines of the *Inferno,* in which Dante and Virgil climb to the light and see the stars again, Fincher's film ends with a gray sky crisscrossed by high-voltage power lines and Mills's execution-style murder of Doe.

*Se7en*'s use of Dante is surprisingly self-conscious throughout, both visually and in its script. Two examples, among many, make this clear. As we follow Somerset's researches in the library early in the film, we are given a long, lingering look at Doré's illustration of *Inferno* 28, in which a sinner holds his decapitated head by the hair. This head, which we see, finds visual echo in the head we don't see in *Se7en,* the severed head of Mills's wife. We see only Somerset's confused and horrified reaction as he opens a package containing the head that has been delivered to him. This reworking of Dante's text could not be more shocking. The respect of homage becomes a kind of reckless search for gruesome effect. But Fincher also handles Dante more lightly. In a memorable scene earlier in the investigation, Mills throws a copy of Dante aside with a burst of profanity. He then thanks an underling for providing him with the Cliffs Notes version of the poem, which he later puts to good use in conversation with Somerset. Dante, it seems, always comes around in *Se7en,* whether one takes a reverential attitude toward his poem or an insolent one.

*Se7en,* like *Beetlejuice,* concentrates on aspects of the *Inferno* itself. The poem's intrinsic features, like Dante's concept of contrapasso or the relation between pilgrim and poet, form the basis for acts of homage and transformation. But a literary text, especially one as dense and suggestive as Dante's poem, has another kind of life in culture: a meaning built up over time that goes beyond its formal features and its themes. Great works of art are both repositories of techniques and ideas as well as touchstones. Subsequent artists (and readers) both draw on them and derive certain standards from them. Audiences and readers can think about what works of art might say in a more immediate sense, but they often step back and think about what such work means in the larger culture.

We can glimpse this in Ridley Scott's 2001 *Hannibal,* in which the creepily charismatic Hannibal Lector (Anthony Hopkins) returns for another game of cat and mouse with agent Clarice Starling (Julianne Moore). Lector's zest for high culture was well established in Jonathan Demme's earlier *Silence of the Lambs* (1991), in which the doctor (Lector) killed and mutilated two policemen to the strains of Bach's *Goldberg Variations.* Part of the shock of this scene lies in the presentation. Lector's mutilation of Sergeant Pembry is as artistic as it is extravagantly horrific. Immediately before the murders, Lector contemplates in evident rapture the lovely opening notes of Bach's piece. He springs to action when the music shifts tempo, handcuffing one officer, spraying the other with Mace and beating him. After the murders, Lector languidly moves his hand over the tiny speaker of his tape recorder as the music slows again. He seems to caress Bach's lilting little air. Of course, what we have yet to see is Pembry's corpse, raised on high to the light for the benefit of the police as they arrive on the scene later. The shock of this sequence partly owes to the distinct recollection of the painter

Francis Bacon's distorted and disturbing portraits (themselves arguably infernal in their recording of life as punishment) in the arrangement of Pembry's body. Lector is insane, but his aesthetic sense is evident, in his acts of both appreciation and creation.

*Hannibal* deepens this disturbing connection between the artistic and the criminal sensibilities. Dante becomes, in the sequel, a cultural touchstone for Lector, who, as the film begins, seeks a permanent position in Florence as a lecturer on the poem. The use of the *Inferno* in the film is less obvious than in *Se7en* but no less pervasive. Hannibal resides in the "Casa Dante," and he gives a lecture on *Inferno* 13. His murders have always had a retributive side, as was evident in the conclusion to the earlier film, in which Lector punctuates a phone call to Clarisse with the offhand mention that he's "meeting an old friend for dinner." Of course, in this case, the old friend is the psychiatrist who presided over Lector's incarceration, a petty, self-serving narcissist, and Lector seems determined to kill and eat him. But the murders in *Hannibal* tend toward the punishments of contrapasso (Lector's encouragement of the self-loathing Adam Verger [Gary Oldman] to cut off pieces of his face, which Lector feeds to a dog; the meticulously decorous meal in which Lector spoon-feeds Paul Krendler's [Ray Liotta] own brains to him). Lector both emulates and champions Dante as a kindred spirit, as one forthright enough to both understand and evaluate the world around him and brave enough to consign certain malefactors to an end that they merit. It is oddly fitting that Lector hides from scrutiny after his escape in a Florence that is, for him, Dante's.

## ADVOCACY AND CRIME:
### MATTHEW PEARL'S *THE DANTE CLUB*

If Lector and, by extension, *Hannibal* make an implicit case for the relevance of Dante in the modern world, Matthew Pearl's best-selling novel, *The Dante Club,* makes this argument quite directly. The novel, set immediately after the American Civil War, imaginatively recasts several Harvard professors and Boston literary figures—among them Oliver Wendell Holmes, James Russell Lowell, George Washington Greene, and J. T. Fields—as amateur detectives. These men, who meet regularly to abet the poet Henry Wadsworth Longfellow in his translation of Dante's *Inferno,* form the club of the book's title.

The plot of *The Dante Club* turns on a series of murders modeled on infernal punishments. Benjamin Galvin, a veteran troubled by the violence he has seen on both sides during the war, has returned to civilian life only to find it largely unchanged by the struggle. Haunted by a sense of injustice, he finds meaning in a chance encounter at a soldiers' aid home, where he hears a member of the Dante Club, George Washington Greene, deliver a sermon fired by Dante's poem. Struck by the parallels between Dante's experience and his own, the traumatized veteran finds order and meaning in the justice of the contrapasso and in the intricacy of God's plan of Hell.

The veteran's disturbed championship of Dante parallels the club's desire to give the poem greater prominence in America. The translation meets determined opposition in the form of Augustus Manning, treasurer of the Harvard Corporation, who seeks to suppress the book by cajoling various club members, suborning a Pinkerton detective to gather information on club members' activities, bribing a local cleric to publish denunciations of the translation, and threatening the translation's publisher. Manning is quite specific about what he does not like about Dante's poem, and this extravagant context allows Pearl to stage wide-ranging arguments about the value of the poet.

So we have an ingenious structure for the novel, one that combines the lurid criminality of a best-seller with a fairly high-minded attempt to reintroduce a literary masterpiece to a wide readership. Part reverence, part shrewd recycling of the poem's memorable punishments, *The Dante Club* embodies the old prescription that literature should both instruct and delight.

Let's examine the delight first. The novel's debt to Dante can be seen even in the way Pearl divides his work into parts: three canticles, recalling Dante's three canticles of the *Inferno, Purgatorio,* and *Paradiso.* This bit of homage runs even deeper. Just as Dante provides a mathematically tidy structure within each canticle (33 cantos to each and 1 prefatory, making yet another shapely figure, 100), Pearl divides each of his canticles into seven chapters. The balance here neatly recalls, without being overly fussy, Dante's intensely ordered presentation.

The murders themselves are fairly straightforward adaptations of Dante's infernal punishments. The first, the execution of a judge, is reported by the maid, who follows a trail of bloodstains, vibrantly colored insects, and false teeth to a fly-blown body. The crime scene has the intensity of a fever-dream:

> Her eyes could not resist making out the nakedness, the wide, slightly hunched back sloping into the crack of the enormous, snowy buttocks, brimming over with the crawling, pallid, bean-shaped maggots above the disproportionately short legs that were kicked out in opposite directions. A solid block of flies, hundreds of them, circled protectively. The back of the head was completely swathed in white worms, which must have numbered in the thousands rather than hundreds.[1]

The effect here is sensational, but the resonance is Dantesque. Near the body, the murderer places "a short wooden staff with a ragged flag, white on both sides" (p. 8), which clinches the connection with the *Inferno.* As we learn later, the killer, enraged by the judge's failure to defend the Dante Club's translation efforts against the Harvard Corporation, has condemned the judge as a neutral, one of "the sorry souls . . . who lived without infamy and without praise" (*Inf.* 3.35–6). Dante's contrapasso here is suggestive: The neutrals, who could not choose in life and remained apart, now must chase a banner for eternity in a long file of equally contemptible sinners. Moreover, however torpid their souls on Earth, in death they feel the spur of endless torment:

> These wretches, who never were alive, were naked and were much stung by gadflies and wasps there, which were streaking their faces with blood that mingled with their tears and was gathered by loathsome worms at their feet. (*Inf.* 3.64–9)

Just as Dante sought to outdo Ovid in his description of the transformation of the thieves in *Inferno* 25 or as Keats vied with Dante in the metamorphosis of Lamia, Pearl seems intent on pushing beyond Dante's efforts. *The Dante Club* builds on Dante's poem, weaving other historical information into the spectacle. The killer learned, from the gruesome firsthand experience of the battlefield, of a species of fly that eats live flesh, not carrion, and he imports such flies for this particular punishment.

The second murder, of the Unitarian minister Elisha Talbot, again allows the killer to filter his experience through Dante's poem. Stung by Talbot's willingness to take a bribe to attack Longfellow's Dante translation in the press, the murderer finds the poem's punishment of simony—the sale of ecclesiastical privileges—to be a fitting template for his vengeance. The simonists, described in *Inferno* 19, make for a memorable exhibition. Confined upside-down in holes in the rock, with flames flickering up and down their feet and legs (their only visible parts), the simonists perform a humiliating, infernal dance. Pearl's killer clubs the minister as he walks through the underground crypt of his church, places him upside-down in a hole he has dug, douses his feet and legs with kerosene, and burns his flesh until it falls from the bones.

Here Pearl's use of the contrapasso is perhaps more interesting than the spectacle of the punishment itself. We learn that the minister has not only offended the murderer by his complicity in attacks on Longfellow's translation, but he has also used his office for profit in other ways. However zealous and upright he now appears, 30 years earlier he was willing to help recruit workers for the railroad with promises of a job and a church community. When the recruits died of overwork and disease, he quietly removed his support from the effort, but he never returned the money he earned. Again, Pearl adheres to Dante's idea of contrapasso, but he embroiders it with a bit of historical fact. If Dante localizes his poem's sinners, so too does Pearl find an American counterpart to the poet's Tuscan malefactors.

Pearl's reuse of Dantesque punishments, while driving the plot, also provides an opportunity for instruction. *The Dante Club* aspires to be a page-turner, but there are moments at which Pearl makes a case for Dante's work that goes beyond deliciously revolting spectacle. The club members themselves, as one might expect in a novel that entwines a real history into its action, speak forcefully about their commitments to their idol Dante.

These commitments mingle high-minded appeals to the public good with more private connections to Dante's poem. Lowell, for instance, ecstatically awaits the publication of the translation as the "discovery of Dante by America" (p. 32). In defending the study of the *Divine Comedy* to the president of Harvard, Lowell provides an expansive national purpose for the poem:

> Shall we have England lord over our bookshelves? Why did we not just hand Lexington over to the redcoats and spare General Washington the trouble of war? . . . Till America has learned to love literature not as an amusement, not as mere

doggerel to memorize in a college room, but for its human-
izing and ennobling energy, my dear reverend president, she
will not have succeeded in that high sense which alone makes
a nation out of a people. That which raises it from a dead
name to a living power. (p. 31)

The question here is a live one: whether America will find its
literary tradition in the Greek and Roman classics (as Manning
insists), as an outgrowth of English literature, or by an affirma-
tive act of choice, in this case, the choice of Dante. And the
issue Lowell raises is more specific than the somewhat general
argument he makes here. In another conversation, one of his
friendly disputes with Holmes, Lowell asserts the peculiar fitness of Dante for this particular moment in history, in which
America, after a terrible war, seeks to find a new order.

Dante's Hell is a part of our world as much as part of the
underworld, and shouldn't be avoided . . . but rather confronted. We sound the depths of Hell very often in this life.
(p. 43)

For Lowell, Dante's situation—that of a returned veteran from
a divisive civil war, one who insists on certain realities being
faced and not simply covered up—is that of postwar America.
Lowell, like other members of the club, speaks from a sense of
mission.

At first such professions of Dantolatry seem like vignettes,
but Pearl carefully connects the enthusiasms of the club with
the murderer's state of mind. Galvin's outrage at the ethical
malaise of postwar Boston fuels his idealization of Dante:

Galvin could not understand how the war could be considered
done. They had not come close to meeting their cause. Slaves
were freed, but the enemy had not changed its ways—had

not been punished. Galvin was not political, but he knew
that the blacks would have no peace in the South, slavery or
no slavery, and he knew also what those who had not fought
the war did not know: that the enemy was all around them at
all times and had not surrendered at all. And never, never for
a moment had the enemy been only the Southerners. (p. 343)

Lowell's abstract insistence on confrontation finds a distorted
counterpart in the experience of this traumatized veteran, and
this shared notion of the importance of confrontation is bound
up, for each, in the figure of Dante. And lest we dismiss Galvin's
faith in Dante as simply an idiosyncratic response to his personal experience, Pearl takes care to remind us that the enthusiasm of club members is not simply the bloodless cogitation of
intellectuals. Longfellow begins his translation after the death
of his wife, and Lowell, although happily remarried, recalls his
first wife as "my Beatrice" in his journal (p. 104).

This mingling of personal and public reappears in the
murderer's application of the contrapassi. Galvin condemns
Healey as a neutral because of his failure to support the translation; others in the book note that Healey infamously took no
stand against the loathsome Fugitive Slave Act, which required
Northern states to return escaped slaves to their so-called mas-
ters. The immediate cause of the murder lay in Galvin's fevered
state of mind, but the novel notes that Healey might well be
considered the natural companion of Dante's arch neutral,
Celestine V, who made the "grand refusal" so despised by the
poet. Similarly, Galvin judges and executes Talbot as a simonist
based on the treachery of his attacks on the Dante translation,
but the novel takes care to point out that the minister's corruption of his clerical office extends beyond the murderer's knowledge. The judgments are curiously fit, all the more so as their
fitness goes beyond the knowledge and intentions of the man
who carries out the punishment.

## DORÉ AND DIY: THE BIRK-SANDERS *INFERNO*

These popular works exploit one aspect of Dante's infernal journey cleverly. In each case, the vision of Hell produces a heightened perception of human corruption. The dark visions of John Doe in *Se7en* and Galvin in *The Dante Club* inspire these men not simply to acts of violence but to acts of *expressive and judgmental* violence. Dante's poem provokes them to make their particular vision of the world visible to others. Hell, as in Eliot's poem, is on Earth; we simply need eyes to see it clearly or, as Lowell puts it, the will to confront it. This rule applies in *Beetlejuice* and *Hannibal* as well. Burton's bureaucratic Hell is a playful extension of everyday life, and Lector finds artistic inspiration suited to his mordant aesthetic wit in the poem's notion of contrapasso. The experience of Dante is a perpetual spur to the renewal of perception.

Put another way, each of these adaptations *invents* the *Inferno*. We use this term advisedly, and we should explain it. Traced to its Latin roots, "invention" is a strange word. A combination of "*in*" (up to, or in) and "*venire*" (to come or arrive), it literally denotes acts of finding or coming upon. Yet it also is taken figuratively to mean acts of contriving or making. The emphasis in the popular adaptations we've discussed so far lies in recognizing the infernal nature of daily life, a Hell on Earth that goes largely unremarked. In works like these, one discovers, at a blow, what has always been there but just out of notice. But in other adaptations of Dante, the emphasis falls on the other meaning of "invention"—on making the reader see in ways that are creative and imaginative. Put another way, we can see Galvin's or Lector's acts as an odd combination of exaggeration (in form) and reduction (in content). Their ways of making others see the Hell on Earth so present to them is through flamboyant and excessive murder. Yet their message is paradoxically reductive: The world becomes grimmer, less capacious, and repetitive. Hell clarifies.

Dante's poem does not have this relentlessly reductive closure. Dante speaks, in the first few lines of the poem, not only of the terrible vision he is about to relate but also of "the good that I found in it," and he concludes the poem with an ascent capped by a wide view of the heavens. Dante's *Inferno* is not simply a judgment on Earth. Although he excoriates his enemies—even entire cities he finds uncongenial—in *Paradiso* 25 he imagines a happy return to Florence, where he would put on the "laurel crown," that is, be honored publicly for his work. We'd like to conclude our discussion of popular adaptations of the poem by exploring this more expansive aspect of Dante's legacy. And in doing so, we'd also like to suggest that the division between high and low culture that we've adhered to in this discussion can, in some instances, prove inadequate.

Sandow Birk's illustrated version of the *Inferno*, published in 2004 and cotranslated by Marcus Sanders, might seem at first glance to hover between not only translation and adaptation but also between reverence and parody. The book provides a new translation of the poem as well as two elaborate drawings for each canto: one prefatory inset and one illustration of Dante's text. Fastidious readers might find Birk's decision to restage Dante's infernal journey in modern Los Angeles (with the entrance to Hell now beneath the freeway) as impudent or disrespectful. (See figure 6.) Other readers might revel in what they perceive as a bit of graffiti art that deflates a tiresome cultural icon. Both reactions would be partially correct, if not simply wrong. Birk's work manages to combine high and low cultures and, like all good adaptations, to turn us back to the original text with renewed appreciation and understanding.

Birk's translation, which he and Sanders term an "adaptation," often revels in street culture. Let's examine the Birk-Sanders version of the encounter with Cerberus, the three-headed

Fig. 6.   Sandow Birk, *Dante at the Gate of Hell,* Courtesy of Koplin del Rio Gallery, Los Angeles.

dog that guards the classical underworld. The original has a raucous quality:

> As the dog that barking craves, and then grows quiet when
> he snaps up his food, straining and struggling only to devour
> it, such became the foul faces of the demon Cerberus, who

so thunders on the souls that they would fain be deaf. (*Inf.*
6.28–33)

This exemplifies what Eliot praised in Dante's poem, its "strong
visual images," its elemental description of unadorned and un-
poetic everyday life. Birk and Sanders go a bit further in their
translation:

> Like the crazed crack addict jonesing for a
> rock who instantly calms down after he scores
> and gets his first drag of smoke,
> Cerberus' disgusting barking heads sniffed
> at the mud and lapped it so intently that
> they seemed oblivious to anything else.[2] (6.29–34)

Although Dante's realism would have been something of a jolt
to readers who approached the poem according to the rules of
the epic, modern audiences might need a bit more juice. Birk and
Sanders bring something of a contemporary urban sensibility to
Dante's comparison, changing the image itself but trying to reproduce the original effect for the reader. The exaggeration they
bring to the adaptation both plays and comments on Dante's
poem. It reminds us that realism like Dante's, however familiar
now, was once an innovation. The adaptation's crack-head Cerberus is at once an act of flamboyance and fidelity to the original.

Birk's illustrations show this unusual combination of vital-
ity and deliberation. In illustrating the poem, Birk invokes Gustave Doré's famous 1861 collection of drawings for the *Inferno*.
(See figure 7.) Doré's illustrations, characterized by an eclectic
mix of Michelangelesque nudes, traditions of landscape sublime
from northern Europe, and elements of popular culture, have
gone through almost 200 editions. As a graphic text, they still
determine how many readers imagine the *Inferno*. Not only
does Birk's homage to Doré's memorable style include echoes of

Fig. 7.   Gustave Doré, *Gate of Hell,* Courtesy of the Division of Rare and Manuscript Collections, Cornell University Library.

formal elements, such as the perspective with which the mouth of Hell is rendered (compare figures 6 and 7), but it also invokes the spirit of Doré's work in its incorporation of popular elements. Both artists seek to engage a wide audience, and neither is bound by restrictive views of aesthetic propriety and taste.

Birk's graphic imagination itself is formidable and intriguing, as is evident in figure 6. Familiar elements of urban life, such as street signs, provide a witty take on Dante's journey. The warning "Do not back up/Severe tire damage" smartly updates the frightening admonition at the gates of Dis, "Abandon every hope, you who enter," as does the helpful advice "More parking lower level," which reminds readers of the enormous capacity of Hell. The ugliness and disorder of the scene—trash in heaps, ragged lines of telephone poles, and graffiti—make the analogy complete. Just as Eliot saw Hell in the crowd of people going over London Bridge, Birk envisions Hell beneath Los Angeles' desolate and soul-destroying freeway system.

This is a familiar move in Dante adaptations, and Birk pursues it through many variations in his illustrations to each canto. But other graphic works in the Birk-Sanders translation (which, for want of a more exact term, we will call visual epigraphs) do not follow the poem in obvious ways. In fact, they seem to form another sequence entirely, one that begins in the "unreal city" of Eliot's imagination but moves beyond this function. Birk provides intricately detailed vignettes: abandoned shopping carts, empty strollers, rubbish left after tagging, a parking meter, a tract home, a Laundromat, a super-size meal, the bleak tables at fast-food establishments. Unlike the panoramic grandeur of the more programmatic illustrations of the poem, these objects or arrangements are carefully separated from context, forcing us to train our attention on these items themselves.

Let's look at the first of these visual epigraphs, in canto 1. (See figure 8.) An abandoned shopping cart, lying on its side in an ill-tended parking lot, the figure does not have obvious relation to the poem's opening lines or, for that matter, the first canto. The details of the drawing—scattered fruit, a few weeds—are spare, and the larger context of the cart is absent. The focus is on the thing itself, the cart, in all its desolation. In fact, the only clear connection to Dante's poem is the prominent display of "Canto I" on the curb.

If the visual epigraphs seem isolated from the poem, the other illustrations in Birk's *Inferno* show abundant and lively connection with the text. If we examine the shopping cart against the other drawing for canto 1 (see figure 9), we are struck by the difference. Birk has taken the opening lines of the poem, the famous "Midway in the journey of our life I found myself in a dark wood, for the straight way was lost" (*Inf.*1.1–3), and rendered them in great detail. Just as Dante localizes his

Fig. 8.   Sandow Birk, Canto 1, *Title Page*, Courtesy of Koplin del Rio
Gallery, Los Angeles.

poem, turning again and again in describing Hell to the world
that he knew, so does Birk localize his version, fitting it to a
modern urban setting. The overriding mood of this rendition
is ironic. The city of the damned has become the city of the
angels, Los Angeles. The pilgrim finds himself lost among tall
buildings, not the forest and trees of Dante's original. A sordid
backstreet succinctly captures the loss of the "right way." The
Birk-Sanders translation echoes the wry humor of the illustration: the "straight way was lost" here becomes an admission by
the pilgrim: "I guess I had taken a few wrong turns."

   One series of illustrations in Birk's adaptation plays a fairly
familiar role in terms of its content. By mapping the action of
the *Inferno* on Los Angeles, Birk follows the tradition of poets like Ezra Pound or T. S. Eliot. Hell, in this reading, is on

Fig. 9.   Sandow Birk, *Dante in the Wilderness*, Courtesy of Koplin del Rio Gallery, Los Angeles.

Earth, if we have eyes to see it, and Dante's poem becomes a way of developing that kind of vision. Just as the journey changes Dante the pilgrim, so does the experience of the poem transform its readers, training them to look beyond habit and convention in order to see deeply into the world. But the question of Birk's choice of graphic style remains to be explored. Although his drawings might be, in this interpretation, a means to an end, they also invite more extended engagement that returns us to the world with a less jaundiced and a less judgmental eye. Birk's cityscapes are often ugly, desolate places; yet, in their careful detail, they call us to the things of this world with more ambivalence. The upturned shopping cart we discussed earlier might be taken as part of the Hell on Earth the other illustrations present. But it also, in its own right, stands as an artistic act in which a part of a disordered urban scene is isolated, reconfigured, and made interesting. There is, even here, the good that Dante insists he found in Hell.

Birk's stance is complex. He revels in the detail and specificity of the urban scene in his visual epigraphs, celebrating the DIY ethos and vibrancy of street art. (See figure 10.) Yet his work invokes Doré—in fact, Birk's *Inferno* might well be seen as an argument for renewed attention to Doré's artistry.

Fig. 10.    Sandow Birk, *Spray Paint Cans,* Courtesy of Koplin del Rio Gallery, Los Angeles.

Nevertheless, perhaps deeper than these allegiances runs yet another argument. Birk's eclectic and popularizing adaptation reminds us that Dante himself imagined a wide audience for his poem. He wrote in the vernacular, not in Latin, moving easily among the abstractions of philosophical doctrine, searching analyses of character, and emotionally charged moments of anguished confession. And most telling of all, Dante's verse moves between the Sweet New Style he and other poets developed for a refined audience of connoisseurs and a raucous language drawn from the streets. Birk's *Inferno,* in spanning so-called high and low cultures, insists that we return to Dante's poem to appreciate Dante's own mingling of styles.

# 8

# Dan Brown's Inferno and the Legacy of Dante

When taking up Dan Brown's *Inferno,* readers might wonder whether they need to know Dante's poem to enjoy the new novel. It's easy to dismiss a concern like this as naive—surely all one needs to know to read a page-turner will be provided by the book itself. Millions of readers who knew nothing about Leonardo raced through the *Da Vinci Code.* Part of Dan Brown's craft is to present facts often known only by specialists thoughtfully and clearly. Nevertheless, the question is a good one. It speaks to something more than the desire for pure sensation. Without dismissing the suspense and pleasure of a good read, the question asks us to think about how curiosity, in the most active and wide sense, might change how we read and how we enjoy literature.

So there are really two answers to this question. You can read the *Inferno* simply for the pleasure of how Brown piques your interest with puzzles and mysteries and then solves them satisfactorily. You can simply go along for the ride. Or you can read more actively, with a curiosity that is less idle than deliberate. The latter method is particularly rewarding, even when applied to a book that works perfectly well when read differently. We've assumed so far that readers want to know more about Dante's poem as well as other adaptations of the *Divine Comedy*, both literary and popular. Armed with such knowledge, readers can then turn or return to Dan Brown's book with a renewed sense of pleasure, both in the way it adapts Dante's poem and how it encourages us to think about Dante's legacy. For every adaptation—even a parody—is an homage that testifies to the greatness of the earlier work.

But we can do more than make assumptions about how knowing Dante's poem might make a difference in reading Brown's *Inferno*. We can compare these two approaches by looking at the opening two sections of the novel: the "Prologue," spoken by Brown's apparent villain, Zobrist, who mysteriously calls himself "the Shade," and Chapter 1. The Prologue traces a very specific itinerary through modern-day Florence from the Arno River to the Badia tower, from which the Shade jumps. Chapter 1 reveals Brown's hero, Robert Langdon, injured and confused as he awakens, much to his surprise, in a hospital just outside Florence. After a break, this chapter cuts to a mysterious—and armed—female figure who stares up at Landon's hospital window as she dismounts a motorcycle. (We'll also include the novel's epigraph condemning "neutrality in times of moral crisis" and the page titled "Fact" that sets out a few guidelines for the reader in this consideration.)

The Prologue, read simply in terms of what Brown provides for us, does everything a page-turner should do. The opening line, "I am the Shade," is perfectly understandable in terms of the information in the Fact section. The Shade thinks of himself moving through a Dantesque underworld trapped between life and death. The Shade's narrative shifts rapidly between the real world of Florence—with its museums and street vendors—and what appears to be a visionary existence of suffering, prophecy, apocalyptic destruction, and persecution. Even readers who had not read Dante's *Inferno* would suspect that the Shade's words, especially those in italics, have something to do with the poet's vision. Phrases like "dolent city" (p. 5) sound antique, and visions of "lustful bodies writhing in fiery rain" (pp. 5–6) or "gluttonous souls floating in excrement" (p. 6) suggest infernal punishments. We needn't understand all these references, any more than we needed to understand Silas's tormented religious ravings in the *Da Vinci Code,* to enjoy the suspense here. In fact, if we've read Brown's previous novels, we can rest assured that we'll be told all we need to know as the plot unfolds.

Nor would any reader of Dan Brown find Chapter 1, which opens with Robert Langdon in an intriguing situation, unfamiliar. Langdon's slow and difficult return to consciousness is full of the puzzles, clues, and teasing references that Brown's other novels have used to keep readers on tenterhooks. The chapter continues the line of infernal allusions begun by the Shade, as Langdon recalls, in fragments, memories of a bloodred river, corpses, and suffering. In fact, his recollections and the visions of the Shade seem to fuse, as Langdon ponders an infernal scene of torment: "hundreds of them now, maybe thousands, some still alive, writhing in agony, dying unthinkable deaths . . . consumed by fire, buried in feces, devouring one another" (p. 9). Just about any reader, primed by the title of the novel, the short description of the *Inferno* provided on the Fact page, and the Shade's apparent hallucinations would connect these references. And readers more attuned to Brown's narrative methods probably would know that Langdon's last formulation of these memories—a veiled woman standing near a river of blood surrounded by corpses—should be kept in mind as one reads on. A puzzle—presumably the first of many—has taken shape, and the solution, as well as the next puzzle, can be expected shortly.

One might note how Brown has connected the Shade and Langdon. Both experience similar visions, albeit for different reasons, and these visions, even to readers unfamiliar with the *Inferno,* would be understood as referring to Dante's poem. The Shade's narrative concludes with his descent into what he terms the "abyss," and Langdon describes his last moments of consciousness before the sedatives take over as being dragged down into a "deep well" (p. 13). Finally, both men make reference to one of Florence's most famous buildings, the Palazzo Vecchio. The Shade, as he moves from the river to the Badia, passes by "the palazzo with its crenellated tower and one-handed clock" (p. 5); Langdon, from his hospital bed, is startled by the sight of "an imposing stone fortress with a notched parapet and a three-hundred-foot tower that swelled near the top, bulging outward into a massive machicolated battlement" (p. 13). We don't know how Langdon and the Shade are linked, but we know the connection has something to do with Dante's poem and the Palazzo Vecchio. The structure here is not subtle, but it creates the suspense necessary to pull readers into the next chapter. These two sections have done their job.

Now let's try an approach to the Prologue and Chapter 1 that assumes some knowledge of Dante's poem. It's worth noting that Dan Brown's choice of title alone suggests that this is appropriate, as does his reference to Dante on the Fact page. Such attention finds reward at once, in the epigraph to the novel: "The darkest places in hell are reserved for those who maintain their neutrality in times of moral crisis."

Readers attuned to Dante's poem will hear echoes of canto 3, where the pilgrim encounters the neutrals: "the sorry souls of those who lived without infamy and without praise" (*Inf.* 3.35–36). Neither evil nor good, hateful to God and to Satan, these beings stood apart during life, and they are cast out of both Heaven and Hell. Brown's reference to the neutrals in so prominent a place—as epigraph—asks that we consider it closely. The epigraph alludes to the poem but embellishes it. The vestibule where the neutrals reside is not one of the "darkest" spots in the *Inferno,* although Dante clearly deems neutrality despicable. The epigraph signals that Brown's use of Dante's poem in the novel will be more active than faithful.

The first words spoken by the Shade in the Prologue open even more possibilities for readers familiar with Dante's poem:

> I am the Shade.
> > Through the dolent city, I flee.
> > Through the eternal woe, I take flight. (p. 5)

This echoes, almost literally, the opening lines of *Inferno* 3. Dante and his guide, Virgil, have reached the Gate of Hell proper, and Dante reads the inscription over it:

> Through me you enter the woeful city,
> Through me you enter eternal grief,
> Through me you enter among the lost. (*Inf.* 3.1–3)

Brown's echo of the original is somewhat more precise than this translation. "Dolent city" sounds a bit old-fashioned, but it renders the Italian *"città dolente"* in a way that makes the allusion more secure. For readers who know their Dante, the Shade's words prompt us to compare his situation with that of Dante the pilgrim in *Inferno* 3.

So where is Dante as he stands before the Gate of Hell? He approaches the river Acheron, surrounded by sighs, lamentations, and cries of the neutrals, those who lived "without infamy and without praise" (*Inf.* 3.36). As the pilgrim approaches the river, he sees the recent arrivals—damned souls waiting to cross into Hell proper in high Greco-Roman style, by means of Charon, the infernal ferryman. Curiously, the poem never specifies how Dante crosses: He faints on the riverbank, awakening on the other side. The line that ends *Inferno* 3 reads "I fell like one who is seized by sleep" (*Inf.* 3.136).

The parallel is not point by point. No good adaptation should be too faithful. The trick here is to transform the original in interesting ways, and Brown, after evoking *Inferno* 3, concludes his prologue with a different kind of fall for the Shade, who jumps from the Badia tower. The parallel continues in the last words of the Shade—"[I] take my final step, into the abyss" (p. 7)—which echoes Dante's situation as he revives in the next canto: "I found myself on the brink of the chasm" (*Inf.* 4.7–8).

Note how these considerations thicken the experience of the novel. The Shade imagines himself as a new Dante, an infernal traveler who retraces the steps of the poet's journey, but in some transformed way. And this explicit parallel suggests a less obvious one, which places Langdon—someone who awakens (from some violence) and steps into an abyss (the stupor of sedatives)—in similar circumstances.

Let's look at other Dantesque elements in the Prologue and Chapter 1. The Shade, after his opening references to the inscription on the Gate of Hell, follows Dante's work closely. As the Shade crosses the bustling Piazza San Firenze, he reminds himself: "Here all hesitation must be left behind" (p. 5)—an exact translation of words spoken by Virgil, Dante's guide through the Inferno, as the two contemplate the Gate of Hell. In the poem, Dante is confused and fearful about the journey ahead, and Virgil seeks to rouse his courage. Here the Shade, also facing a portal—"the iron gate at the base of the stairs" (p. 5)—makes his retracing of Dante's steps emphatic.

In fact, the Shade sees himself as Dante. Just down the page in Brown's Prologue we find him aligning himself yet again with the poet, this time with Dante's life. "Ungrateful land!" (p. 5) recalls many passages in the *Inferno* where Dante bitterly denounces his fellow Florentines. The Prologue continues with a barrage of Dantesque visions: "As I climb, the visions come hard . . . the lustful bodies writhing in fiery rain, the gluttonous souls floating in excrement, the treacherous villains frozen in Satan's icy grasp" (pp. 5–6). Each of these images points to a specific passage in the poem. The lustful appear in canto 5, pummeled by winds; the gluttons, harassed by Cerberus, endure a cold and everlasting rain in canto 6; and the last region of Hell, Cocytus, harbors traitors of several kinds, some immersed in ice up to their neck, others being flayed and eaten by Satan. These are memorable torments, chosen for their value as spectacle, and they work perfectly well to establish the Shade's state of mind as he climbs the stairs. But a reader familiar with Dante's poem might notice something else. Brown's references are all a bit askew. The fiery rain does not torment the lustful, although the blasphemers, sodomites, and usurers in cantos 15 and 16 do endure this punishment. The gluttons are not "floating in excrement," although the rain they endure is foul enough to make the earth stink; submersion in excrement is the fate of the flatterers in *Inferno* 18. And the last image seems to confuse punishments to the treacherous. Some are indeed frozen, but only three archtraitors are eaten by Satan (Judas, Cassius, and Brutus), and these three do not seem to be frozen.

The differences between the Shade's visions and Dante's poem raise interesting questions for readers. We could dismiss these allusions as errors on Brown's part. But it could well be that we should understand them as mistakes made by the Shade or a reworking of the poem by this avenger in what seems to be his last few frenzied minutes of life. The Shade's next reference to Dante, as he stands above Florence on the tower, has a similar imprecision: "Far below is the blessed city that I have made my sanctuary from those who exiled me" (p. 6). Florence, in fact, exiled Dante, and although the poet fondly recalls the church where he was baptized in *Inferno* 19, he more frequently disparages his native city as fractious, indecent, and decadent. The Shade twists Dante's poem to his own uses, remaining true to its spirit but not its literal language. Whether slips or signs, the Shade's use of Dante's poem attracts our attention.

Robert Langdon's confused return to consciousness in Chapter 1 also features recognizable allusions to Dante's poem. As in the case of the Shade's visions, there is a certain imprecision to the references. Moreover, Langdon (and, of course, Dan Brown) adds elements to the poem:

> Langdon took a step toward the river, but he could see the waters were bloodred and too deep to traverse. When Langdon raised his eyes again to the veiled woman, the bodies at her feet had multiplied. There were hundreds of them now, maybe thousands, some still alive, writhing in agony, dying unthinkable deaths . . . consumed by fire, buried in feces, devouring one another. He could hear the mournful cries of human suffering echoing across the water. (p. 9)

This passage evokes but also builds on the *Divine Comedy*. "Consumed by fire" has many possible references in the poem, from the heretics burning in their tombs (*Inf.* 9 and 10), to the rain of fire that punishes the blasphemers, sodomites, and usurers (*Inf.* 15 and 16), to the simonists roasting upside-down (*Inf.* 19), to the fires that enclose the false counselors (*Inf.* 26). "Buried in feces" is more specific, referring to the flatterers immersed in excrement (*Inf.* 18). "Devouring one another" is quite exact: In Cocytus, the traitor Ugolino chews on the head of his enemy, the archbishop who betrayed him. But the most precise reference comes later in Langdon's reverie: "a writhing pair of legs, which protruded upside down from the earth, apparently belonging to some poor soul who had been buried

headfirst to his waist" (pp. 9–10). This punishment is easily located in Dante: It is the fate of the simonists, church figures who
sold spiritual goods or ecclesiastical office. Langdon's memory
of this vision, however, adds one mysterious element—the letter "R" written on the sufferer's thigh. Again, the presentation
asks readers to link the Shade and Langdon, both of whom call
up Dante's poem but also supplement it.

So Brown, through references to Dante's *Inferno,* has
aligned the two men. We can also examine other connections that are forged around the material from Dante. Foremost among these would be the additional material in Langdon's memories—most insistently the mysterious presence of a
"veiled woman" who stands "on the banks of a bloodred river
surrounded by bodies" (p. 13). This points to *Inferno* 12, in
which murderers are immersed in a boiling river of blood. This
image connects Dantesque visions of punishment and suffering
with a new feature. Brown complicates this figure with other
details—an amulet decorated by a snake coiled about a staff,
a tainia cloth. The snake refers to the Rod of Asclepius, which
in Greek mythology is associated with healing and medicine.
A tainia cloth, also from the Greek tradition, is a band worn
around the head and also used to decorate monuments of the
dead. So the vision becomes a mixture of Dantesque and classical elements, which, after all, is itself in the tradition of Dante's
poem. The *Inferno* frequently blends elements of Christian and
Greco-Roman cultures—perhaps most strikingly in its use of a
pagan poet, Virgil, to guide the pilgrim on a Christian journey.
At this point in the novel, we don't yet know how Brown's
amalgamation of sacred and profane works, but we have seen a
similar presentation in Dante.

Ultimately, knowing more about Dante deepens our engagement with Brown's book. Instead of simply waiting for the
solution to the riddles posed by the story, readers are encour-
aged to take a more active role in the story—we create some of

the suspense ourselves by noting details not made explicit by the narrative.

## READING THE GAPS

This is a powerful way to read—one that begins in what a book discloses but freely builds on it. No reading is a simple decoding. One does not simply reduce a story to a simpler and more compact meaning. Every work of art has gaps that readers must fill. In making these inevitable inferences, the important thing is to be conscious of the process.

Let's examine another instance where we might add to the pleasure of what Brown's book discloses by recalling the experience of Dante's poem. Dante's underworld journey has a double function: It shows the living what the afterlife might be, but it also reminds readers of dystopic elements of life on Earth. It is at once prophecy and jeremiad. Zobrist, in making his case for an overpopulation crisis, follows many authors in the Dantesque tradition by combining these two functions. In his presentation to Elizabeth Sinskey, the director of the World Health Organization, he insists that overpopulation will make Earth a Hell:

> Under the stress of overpopulation, those who have never considered stealing will become thieves to feed their families. Those who have never considered killing will kill to provide for their young. All of Dante's deadly sins—greed, gluttony, treachery, murder, and the rest—will begin percolating . . . rising up to the surface of humanity, amplified by our evaporating comforts. We are facing a battle for the very soul of man. (p. 103)

Later, Zobrist's vision of Hell on Earth takes another form. The clue he devises for Sinskey, the cylinder seal, contains a device that projects Botticelli's Map of Hell. But Zobrist's version of the map has been modified. Zobrist rearranges a particular section of the map, adding the letters that spell "*cerca trova*" and inserting a version of himself—a figure wearing a Venetian plague mask—as well. These changes emphasize a specific part of Hell: the eighth circle, or Malebolge. This region, divided into ten ditches, holds those guilty of various kinds of fraud. This is a clever clue—visually striking and witty at once—but there are many horrific sections in the *Inferno,* and we might ask why Zobrist favors Malebolge.

We are, of course, on our own here: Brown does not raise this question explicitly. But it's one that active readers might well ask, and it offers a space for readers to enlarge Brown's presentation by their own creative efforts. Why would the sins and punishments of Malebolge, of fraud, be more fitting for Zobrist's apocalyptic vision than other kinds of sin in Dante's poem?

To answer this, we need to think about the structure of Dante's Hell. The poet gives it almost excessive organization—in fact, it displays several overlapping patterns. There are nine circles, of course. But three main divisions cut across these circles, denoting and separating the sins of incontinence, violence, and fraud. Malebolge is a part of Lower Hell. When Zobrist emphasizes this kind of sin, as opposed to the sins of incontinence (lust, gluttony, avarice, prodigality, wrath) or of violence (tyrants, murderers, suicides, blasphemers, usurers, sodomites), he follows Dante in his consideration of the damned.

For modern readers, Dante's judgment of these sins is hard to understand. Why should a sin like flattery or theft be worse than murder or tyranny? Dante, however, is very clear about the reasons for this surprising ranking of evils. In *Inferno* 11, Virgil explains the structure of Hell to the pilgrim by carefully noting significant differences between the consequences of fraud and those of incontinence or violence:

> Fraud, which gnaws every conscience, a man may practice
> upon one who trusts in him, or upon one who reposes no
> confidence. This latter way seems to sever only the bond of
> love which nature makes . . . (*Inf.* 11.52–6)

Dante here follows several philosophers, principally Aristotle (through Arabic sources) and Thomas Aquinas. The distinction he borrows is subtle but suggestive. Fraud, unlike incontinence and violence, has ramifications for the entire community, breaking the "bond of love" that naturally exists among men. Fraud strikes at the basis of trust necessary to society. Hence Dante considers it a far worse sin. So when Zobrist imagines a Hell on Earth produced by overpopulation, he imagines it in terms of a widespread breakdown, the kind of savagery punished in Malebolge.

Zobrist does not conjure up a vision of a crisis that leads people simply to seek pleasures like sex, or overeating, or wasting money. He thinks of the more cold-blooded pursuit of advantage. Fraud takes planning: it is not an opportunistic act, conceived in the heat of the moment. It is the merciless calculation of Venedico Caccianemico, who pimps his sister for the Marquis of Este. It is the systematic atmosphere of duplicity built up over time by flatterers like Alessio Interminei. It is exemplified by the grasping Pope Nicholas III, who sells his office to benefit his family. It is the pervasive criminality of the barrators from Lucca, a city where "everyone is a grafter" (*Inf.* 21.41). It is the rebellious and violent fraud of Vanni Fucci, who steals church relics and, in Malebolge, gives the medieval equivalent of the finger (the fig) to God.

Perhaps the last ditch of Malebolge most powerfully sketches the social breakdown that widespread fraud brings. Here we find falsification on the most basic levels: falsification of metals, of persons, of currency, and of words. These are, of course, the essential levels of social exchange. To strike at the currency of money, identity, or language effectively reduces life to a state of nature—a violent struggle of one against all. Dante concludes his journey through Malebolge with a darkly humorous interlude, in which the counterfeiter Master Adam, immobilized by a kind of dropsy, exchanges insults and blows with the equally immobile Sinon, betrayer of the Trojans, who suffers from a stinking fever. In the background, as a kind of savage counterpoint to their pathetic violence, are two other damned sinners, these counterfeiters of persons, "two pallid shades that I saw biting and running like the pig when it is let out of the sty" (*Inf.* 30. 25–7). This combination of bestial violence, rancor, and disgusting illness makes a memorable conclusion to Dante's tour of the eighth circle.

It remains to readers to recollect these features of Dante's text in considering Brown's. If we do, we can enlarge Brown's presentation as well as our pleasure in the live connection we establish between the novel and the rich tradition it invokes. Zobrist often refers to Dante's prescience, his genius, but it falls to readers to follow his hints.

## ZOBRIST'S INFERNO: "OUR DANCE HAS BEGUN"

There are several moments in Brown's novel where we might follow references to Dante in engaging ways. But Brown's use of Dante does not stop here, with these invitations to creative reading. The links he establishes to the *Divine Comedy* are far more ingenious. Dante's poem does not simply provide a visual repertoire for readers. It offers a conceptual model for the central action of the novel. It is not simply Brown as author who employs Dante and the Dantesque tradition; the villain of the piece, Bertrand Zobrist, makes the boldest use of the poem and its legacy.

Tradition is a complex thing. Bob Dylan put it well when he received a lifetime Grammy Award a few years ago. He turned the statuette over in his hands a few times and then he said tantalizingly, "This reminds me of something my daddy used to say." He then waited, for what seemed forever on television—maybe seven or eight seconds—and then added, "Well, my daddy said a lot of things." This is an astute meditation on tradition by an artist who has exploited various musical traditions brilliantly. Tradition is like a kind of parent, and, like Dylan's father, it says a lot of things, never just one.

The tradition of writing in the legacy of Dante's *Inferno* has a similar complexity. To invoke Dante, at least beyond simply recalling images from the poem, has meant different things at different times. Many writers have seized on the prophetic aspects of the *Divine Comedy*: Dante's denunciation of political injustice and religious corruption, and his projection of a better social and spiritual order. For instance, just about any poem written in terza rima, Dante's signature verse form, in the first half of the nineteenth century in Britain builds on this tradition of prophecy. When Percy Bysshe Shelley wants to announce a revolutionary movement that will sweep away old ways of thinking in his short lyric poem "Ode to the West Wind," he uses terza rima. Similarly, in 1819, when his contemporary, Lord Byron, wants to rouse the English public to protest the miserable political situation in Italy, he produces "The Prophecy of Dante," a poem that employs both Dante's rhyme scheme and his division of the poem into cantos. Such uses of Dante don't simply reference or sample his poem. They invoke the *Divine Comedy* to intervene—to do something with the poem, to speak through it, and to bend its force toward some new object.

Let's look closely at how Brown uses Dante in the book. The character most closely associated with the *Divine Comedy* is Zobrist, who refers to the poem in nearly every scene he's involved in. Zobrist's plot is a simple one. Angered by Sinskey's incomprehension and opposition, he produces a "clever little barb fashioned from a bone" designed to lead her to the release site of the virus. The clues he leaves are fairly straightforward. Langdon had pretty well resolved them before his induced amnesia. The bone cylinder seal contains a projector that provides a modified version of Botticelli's Map of Hell. The rearrangement of figures in one particular section of the map, Malebolge, produces a scrambled phrase, *cerca trova,* and another addition to the map indicates that "the truth can be glimpsed only through the eyes of death." The first of these clues leads to Vasari's painting in the Palazzo Vecchio; the second points to Dante's death mask, held in a small chamber directly opposite the words on the Vasari painting. The mask, like the map, has been modified: seven "P"s have been added to the back. When erased, in a clever reenactment of a scene from *Purgatory* (9.112–114), another clue is visible—this in the form of circular writing. The passage begins with a citation from *Inferno* 9 ("O you who have sound understanding" [61]) but continues with an adaptation of elements of Dante's poem. The clues now point to a treacherous doge who decapitated horses and "plundered the bones of the blind." The solution here is only mildly problematic. Langdon is led to the tomb of Enrico Dandolo in Istanbul, where he finds the nearly dissolved remnants of the container of the vector virus Zobrist has released. Other puzzles are introduced as Langdon works his way from Florence to Venice to Istanbul, such as Busoni's dying reference to the opening of *Paradiso* 25, but they are produced by others intent on either aiding Langdon or retarding his inquiry.

Although this plot superficially recalls earlier novels by Brown, it's noteworthy that it differs significantly from them. *The Da Vinci Code* concerns the rediscovery of historical fact long suppressed by a powerful organization—the Catholic Church. There is an objective quality to Langdon's recovery of various historical events, and his pursuit of this truth

constitutes the plot of the novel. In Brown's *Inferno,* the plot
is a creation of Zobrist, his "barb." We proceed, according to
Zobrist's scheme, to *his* truth, not to some more general truth
about the world. Even though we are led to think that Sinskey,
Langdon, Sienna Brooks, and even the provost act to prevent
the release of the virus, we discover that the release has already
transpired before the hunt begins. The entire plot is Zobrist's
creation: part revenge on Sinskey, who has pursued and tormented him for a year, and part pride, as he'd like to be known
for his Inferno—his gift to humanity.

Zobrist is then, in a strange way, akin to the author of the
book. He sets the plot's broad outlines, and he ensures that it
will be set in motion. It is Zobrist who takes up and exploits the
Dantesque tradition. As he tells Sinskey after their confrontation, "Then it appears our dance has begun" (p. 140)—but it
is a dance with the reader as well. The entire plot of Brown's
*Inferno* leads to a consideration of Zobrist's ideas about population. Zobrist's ultimate act is biological terrorism, but what
precedes his release of the vector virus is more like an exposi-
tion, or even a kind of persuasive argument. His video takes
an audience in the book—Sinskey, then Langdon and others—
through a process that forces them to confront a problem that
has been suppressed and to confront it in terms that Zobrist
himself sets. Dante sets himself up as prophet in the *Divine
Comedy,* but Zobrist goes further, asserting in his video: "But I
am not a prophet. I am your salvation" (p. 43).

One might, reading quickly, simply class Zobrist as one in
a long line of pop-culture villains bent on some sort of world
domination or vendetta—a version of the mad scientist in *Dr.
No* or Drax in *Moonraker.* But reading more carefully, it's clear
that Brown takes much care in his presentation of his villain—
to the point of partially rehabilitating him in the final chapters
of the novel. It's easy, in the breathless conclusion of Brown's
*Inferno,* to miss a striking reversal by Sinskey:

> I may disagree with Bertrand's methods, but his assessment
> of the state of the world is accurate. This planet is facing
> a serious overpopulation issue. If we manage to neutralize
> Bertrand's virus without a visible alternate plan . . . we are
> simply back at square one. (p. 452)

Given the ferocity of her opposition to and the tenacity of her
pursuit of Zobrist, this is an astonishing change in attitude. Recall Sinskey's response to Zobrist in their meeting: She brands
him, by turns, "criminal," "mad," "insane," and "lunatic,"
and she concludes by informing him "I consider this a terrorist
threat and will treat it as such" (p. 140). Yet here, after following Zobrist's cues to the end in Istanbul's city cistern, Sinskey
has accepted his assessment of the population crisis. In fact, she
hints that she might well argue that Zobrist's "gift" be accepted. Without an alternative response to the situation, she seems
unwilling to undo the work of the virus. She seems, unexpectedly, to have become a convert to Zobrist's Malthusian vision
and a reluctant supporter of his plan.

Here we might step back a minute to note another strange
twist to the plot of the novel. Everything that has transpired in
the book has been, we now learn, futile. We've been following
Langdon—and later Sinskey, Bruder, and the provost as they
join forces—in a race to save the world from biological terrorism. But Zobrist, by releasing the virus before the action of the
novel began, has ensured that these heroic actions are point-
less. When he threw himself from the Badia tower, the dispersal
of the agent had already begun. What remains is his barb, his
revenge on Sinskey and the explanation of his action. The frantic decoding of clues and the desperate chase are not so much
to save the world as to understand what Zobrist has made
of it. The only action that matters in the novel is Zobrist's;
everyone else simply follows his lead. Moreover, in a strange
twist of events, the reader finds that all the suspense is illusory.

Everything significant in the book has already happened by the time Langdon wakes up in Florence. However heroic his actions in earlier Brown novels, such as in *Angels and Demons,* where he acts decisively to save the cardinal who eventually becomes the new pope, Langdon is ultimately irrelevant to the action of the *Inferno.*

Now we can see how clever Brown's use of Dante has been. Zobrist takes up the tradition of Dante, first in ways that seem ludicrous but, as the novel progresses, in ways that become plausible. He faces a problem, the denial that so conspicuously greets his warnings about overpopulation, and he finds, in Dante's poem, a way of making his concerns persuasive, both in terms of the looming crisis, which he likens to the punishments of the *Inferno,* and in terms of his solution, which mimics the path Dante charts to salvation, that the way down is in fact the way up. Langdon correctly notes this, even before he comes to accept Zobrist's vision, when he thinks, as he deciphers the spiral of verses on the death mask, "Zobrist may have been a lunatic . . . but he certainly had a sophisticated grasp of Dante" (p. 280).

When we first encounter Zobrist, as the harassed Shade of the Prologue, we read his Dante-inspired thoughts simply as madness. Once we finish the book, we might read them as a complicated mix of lucidity and insanity. We can trace this in Zobrist's own comments about Dante. In Chapter 17 the provost recalls his last meeting with his client. Once an impressive figure, Zobrist is now harried and disheveled. He has new instructions for the head of the Consortium—that he deliver his barb to Sinskey and upload a video globally—as well as a gift for the provost himself. This item, a "massive" edition of the *Divine Comedy,* reflects the nature of Zobrist's engagement with Dante's vision. "[T]his book was written *for* me" (p. 76), announces Zobrist, and his annotation on the first page of the poem explains how. The opening three lines of the *Inferno* appear, written in calligraphy: "Midway upon the journey of our life / I found my-self within a forest dark, / for the straightforward pathway had been lost" (p. 77). This famous tercet, richly suggestive, sets out Dante the pilgrim's situation—conscious, all at once, of the collapse of any purpose in his life and unsure what path to take in a menacing world. By presenting himself as an everyman, Dante asks us to apply this capacious model, in which the "straightforward path" can be regained only by a counterintuitive measure. One must go down to go up; one must go through Hell in order to get to Paradise. Zobrist adopts the model and applies it to his own life in his own way. More importantly, he generalizes the lesson, applying it to humankind.

Zobrist's reading of Dante seems obsessive and maniacal when we first encounter it, but as the novel develops, his charge that the world is in denial about the population crisis becomes more plausible. Moreover, as Langdon notes, Zobrist does understand the poem's power. In his video, he declares ominously—but credibly—"Dante's hell is not fiction . . . it is prophesy!" (p. 144). If one accepts Zobrist's view of the population crisis, this is an astute use of the poem as well as the tradition of the poem that writers have helped to develop over the past 700 years. Zobrist follows other apocalyptic thinkers who have noted that Dante's poem describes not simply Hell but a Hell on Earth. Hell is not only in the underworld; it is in Dante's Italy. As the damned souls tell their stories, the sins they describe reveal that life on Earth is just as horrific as the experience of Hell—that the world, like the Inferno, is full of damned and tormented souls. Dante's poem does not ask that we make the pilgrim's exact journey; it asks that we recognize that an infernal landscape is already all around us.

Zobrist's particular vision is a variant of this traditional reading of Dante's poem. His Malthusian, nightmarish future envisions a world in which the dearth of resources not only starves but demoralizes humans. Whatever "virtue and brotherhood" humans display depends on the food supply. Once the food supply becomes grossly inadequate, "Dante's nine-ringed hell" (p. 144) becomes a lived reality.

Zobrist's use of Dante is fairly straightforward, however fanatical. His tantalizing clue, *cerca trova,* could easily sum up his relation to the poem. For Zobrist, the *Divine Comedy* provides a pattern for his own experience—just as the poem has done across the centuries for other readers. It is a kind of master text that explains his struggles. For instance, the pilgrim's confusion in the dark wood and his loss of the right path offer suggestive parallels to Zobrist's own situation. The scientist, once he finds moral certainty about the danger of unchecked population growth, also finds his path out of confusion. He invents a means to prevent the looming crisis. Zobrist, also like Dante, has his own Beatrice figure in the devoted Sienna Brooks. But above all, Zobrist adopts Dante's role as prophet, seeking to stir a torpid and uncomprehending audience to act. The quotation from the *Inferno* that Zobrist builds on for the circular riddle on the back of the death mask is significant. He quotes Dante in the act of calling to "sturdy intellects," those who can read what is hidden or obscure—in other words, those who are no longer in denial about difficult but important truths.

## DAN BROWN'S *INFERNO*

Dan Brown's relation to Dante—as well as to Zobrist's mission—is more complicated. Brown's comments on his book have been fairly bland. "My hope for this book is that people are inspired either to discover or rediscover Dante. And, if all goes well, they will simultaneously appreciate some of the incredible art that Dante has inspired for the last 700 years." In speaking of the book's theme, he declared, "This is not an activist book. I don't have any solution. This is just my way of saying, 'Hello, there's an issue that people far more skilled than I am in these topics need to address.'"[1] Yet the book itself speaks somewhat differently. One might say that Brown has created a novel that makes an unexpectedly passionate argument about a crisis, in richly Dantesque terms, but that allows him some distance from this advocacy.

First of all, let's recall how Brown changes the presentation of the crisis that inspires Zobrist. We first see Zobrist as the "Shade," a frantic and suicidal madman for whom Dante's poem has become as real as the streets of Florence through which he passes. His overheated rhetoric, mixing quotations from the poem, events from Dante's life, delusional grandeur, and seeming paranoia, tags him as a villain almost at once. Our next extended encounter with Zobrist comes in Chapters 9 and 10, when facilitator Knowlton, troubled by the video Zobrist left for release, ponders whether he should show it to the provost. Brown carefully frames this first glimpse at the video, emphasizing the menacing qualities of the production. The bag containing the vector virus could not be more eerie: it holds "some kind of gelatinous, yellow-brown liquid" which we later learn is "amorphous," "distended," and "murky." The contents of the bag "swirl slowly, like the eye of a silently growing storm" (p. 42). Zobrist's appearance could not be more ominous—first as shadow, then as "misshapen," and finally as "half bird," that is, seemingly possessed of a beak rather than a nose. His message, at once defensive, self-righteous, wounded, and threatening, has all the distinctive features of the evil genius, as his conclusion to the video makes clear:

> "And so I stand, deep within this cavern, gazing out across the lagoon that reflects no stars. Here in this sunken palace, Inferno smolders beneath the waters.
>
> Soon it will burst into flames.
>
> And when it does, nothing on earth will be able to stop it." (p. 48)

Also noteworthy here is the combination of melodrama and cliché in Zobrist's rhetoric. This is not the first pop-culture villain who speaks from a cavern threatening widespread and inevitable death.

Zobrist's next appearance in the novel (Chapter 17), in the provost's memories of his last interview with his client, does nothing to change the impression left by the Prologue and the video. The provost recalls a changed man, whom he first encountered as "a notable figure in his field . . . clean cut, and exceptionally tall," now "disheveled" and "wild-eyed" (p. 73). Zobrist's new requests trouble the provost, and his gift of the *Divine Comedy* disconcerts him.

It's worth noting, even here, that Brown does not so much present Zobrist as a man but as other characters' impressions of him. Zobrist exists in recollections, not in the more direct way that other characters in the book come to us. Brown moves easily among characters in his novel, dipping into their thoughts as well as presenting their words and actions. Our picture of Zobrist, however, at least after the first pages of the novel, is always *someone's* picture.

That picture begins to change as the novel develops. Elizabeth Sinskey, the director of the World Health Organization (WHO), provides the next glimpse of Zobrist. As he does with the video, Brown parcels out the meeting between Sinskey and the scientist in bits and over time, in Chapters 22 and 31. Of course, such fragmentation creates suspense in the narrative, but we should also think of other effects that delaying information might have. Brown shows great care in the way he develops Zobrist, and we might, as readers, heed this as we think of the novel.

Sinskey, dizzy and breathing with difficulty from vertigo, recalls being summoned by Zobrist. The scientist, with scant ceremony, gives her a condescending lecture (one that relies on an image from the artist Gustave Doré as well as statistical evidence) on the history of population growth, and he ridicules the efforts of the WHO to combat the danger. The exchange ends (in Chapter 31) with Sinskey declaring that she will report Zobrist as a "potential bioterrorist" (p. 140), a conclusion that fits Zobrist into the familiar scenario of mad villain. But a closer look at the presentation suggests that Brown is not simply evoking this stereotype. Zobrist is not Dr. No; his arguments are not those of a madman bent on world domination. In fact, Sinskey assents, albeit silently, to the case that his graphs and his arguments make. When she objects to his ridicule of the WHO's efforts to promote birth control, his counter argument, that these have only provoked massive efforts by the Catholic Church against contraception, effectively silences her. She does not contest Zobrist's graph showing exponential population growth, and she admits, to herself, that this familiar chart "always brought an eerie sense of inevitability" (p. 103). When Zobrist mentions Machiavelli's quotation about overpopulation, Sinskey provides it in full. Much of this exchange is less a debate than an accord.

Chapter 22 ends with Zobrist in high villain mode. When Sinskey counters the scientist's estimate of the optimum world population with a snippy "it's a little late for that," Zobrist's response, a terse "Is it?" (p. 105), seems to place him with other intransigent madmen in popular fiction. But when Sinskey's recollections of the scene continue, nine chapters later, we again find her without compelling counter arguments. Her response to another of Zobrist's graphs, one developed by her own organization, is a combination of "helplessness" and acceptance. She herself concedes (again, to herself) "this graph painted a chilling picture not of the distant future . . . but of the very *near* future" (p. 138; emphasis in original). The end of the chapter again puts a villainous turn on Zobrist, as Sinskey warns him that she'll report him as a potential terrorist, but it's worth recalling that he does not suggest that the overpopulation problem be corrected with mass extermination. Certainly readers, following earlier cues in the novel that Zobrist is a madman, might think that he proposes such measures. But one might also recall that this is Sinskey's account of the meeting, not an objective presentation of the encounter. And Sinskey recalls this meeting as she works to prevent what she thinks is a terrorist attack. Brown's presentation, which elicits Sinskey's accusations and her righteous anger, misleads readers—ever so slightly, but, as we shall argue, purposefully.

The shift in Brown's presentation of Zobrist begins in Chapter 38, between bouts of Sinskey's delirium. As she arrives at the airport after her meeting with Zobrist, she receives a handwritten note from her new adversary: "The darkest places in hell are reserved for those who maintain their neutrality in times of moral crisis" (p. 163). From Sinskey's perspective, at that moment, such a message confirms that, as Zobrist had said earlier, their "dance has begun" (p. 140). The missive is perfectly comprehensible as the taunting humor of a villain. But Brown complicates this interpretation considerably. This is not the first time that these words have appeared in the novel: They are, word for word, the epigraph to Brown's *Inferno* as well. This echo is worth careful consideration. Epigraphs usually stand as an outside comment on the literary work that follows. In this instance, the epigraph seems to lend support to the villain of the piece, which, at the very least, gives him more prominence, if not a kind of authority in the novel.

We should trace this quotation further. Zobrist repeats this charge in his video, which we might well expect. But Brown adds yet another repetition, in the Epilogue, and this repetition is made by the character who for most of the novel has seemed the hero—our intrepid symbologist Robert Langdon. As he returns to Boston and Harvard, musing on his adventures, the professor not only quotes Zobrist but also affirms his diagnosis of crisis. "For Langdon, the meaning of these words had never felt so clear: *In dangerous times, there is no sin greater than inaction*" (p. 463; emphasis in original). More telling is Langdon's next admission:

> Langdon knew that he himself, like millions, was guilty of this [inaction]. When it came to the circumstances of the world, denial had become a global pandemic. Langdon promised himself that he would never forget this. (p. 463)

Here Brown clinches a long and surprising argument, one that revises Zobrist's role in the book. Langdon recognizes his denial, finds his "inaction" (which he, like Zobrist, terms a "sin" and not a secular failing) distasteful, and resolves not to forget. This change in perspective asks the reader to think again of Zobrist's arguments, to consider them in the terms that he presents them—to, as Sienna puts it, confront these horrors as "not impossible, . . . just *unthinkable*" (p. 214).

As we've seen, the first half of the novel frames Zobrist's arguments in ways that ensure that readers dismiss them. But the second half of the book, while not entirely undoing the effects of the initial presentation of the scientist's ideas, presents them more objectively. The first of these more even-handed treatments comes, implausibly, in Chapter 50, as Sienna and Langdon, having just taken the Duke of Athens stairway out of the Palazzo Vecchio, emerge, in ludicrous disguise, on the street. As they walk toward the Casa di Dante (the Dante museum in Florence), where Langdon hopes to find a copy of the *Divine Comedy* so that he can solve yet another next clue, the professor strikes up an impromptu conversation. Sienna then informs Langdon of Zobrist's work on population. Her account of the scientist's ideas is frank; he has asked questions that range from the uncomfortable to the despicable. But Langdon is shocked to find that Sienna considers his main point, that a crisis of population looms, correct. Again, we might note Brown's technique here. Langdon's objections—which, later in the novel, thinking back, he himself will consider to be denial, not sober analysis—provide an opportunity for a short lecture by Sienna on overpopulation. Not only does she lay out Zobrist's case, she takes pains to explain why his argument is resisted so fiercely. Yet again, this exchange is less debate than persuasion. Although Langdon, like Sinskey before him, initially resists Zobrist's analysis, he too accepts and even affirms some of these ideas. In fact, Langdon goes further than Sinskey: Where the director of WHO assented silently as she listened to Zobrist, Langdon embellishes and extends Sienna's argument. His reaction to her words is significant: "Langdon exhaled, trying to process everything he had just heard" (p. 215). Note how subtly Brown has shifted the presentation of Zobrist's ideas. Langdon does not dismiss Zobrist's alarms as simple villainy. He pauses, he considers. The second half of the conversation shows Langdon increasingly sympathetic to Zobrist's alarms, at times even anticipating the scientist's conclusions as Sienna presents his arguments.

The conversation closes with a hypothetical question that Langdon cannot answer. Sienna concludes by asking a version of British philosopher Philipa Foot's famous "trolley problem":

> "Zobrist asked the following: If you could throw a switch and randomly kill half the population on earth, would you do it?"
>
> "Of course not."
>
> "Okay. But what if you were told that if you *didn't* throw the switch right now, the human race would be extinct in the next hundred years?" She paused. "Would you throw it then?" (p. 218)

Langdon is stumped, and rather than answering the question, he notes that they've arrived at their destination. His relieved "We're here" is balanced by Sienna's "Like I said. *Denial*" (p. 219). This is a key exchange in Brown's presentation of Zobrist. Unlike earlier scenes, the presentation here of the scientist's ideas is neutral. There is less heat, less outrage. We've come a long way from the earlier accounts of Zobrist as mad villain. Sienna, Zobrist's proxy in the argument, clearly gets the better of Langdon here, reducing him to evasion.

This is not to say that there are no answers to the trolley problem. But Brown decides not to explore them. This decision provides a clear line of development for his novel, one that begins with a villain with a mad plan but that revises this assessment gradually as the story progresses. Zobrist is not made heroic or even fully rehabilitated, but Brown does ask that his ideas on population be considered carefully. Perhaps more forcefully, he shows us, as in the last exchange between Langdon and Sienna, the depth of denial that precludes our understanding of the situation. Brown tells us about overpopulation, but he shows us denial.

Brown's plot continues this return to Zobrist's ideas, amid much suspense and pursuit, but the terms of these reconsiderations have changed. In Chapter 67, when Sinskey recalls a conversation she had with Langdon on the plane ride to Florence, the emphasis falls on Zobrist's plans rather than his analysis of the situation. Both Sinskey and Langdon condemn the means that Zobrist has chosen to rectify the crisis, but not so much the ends. Both object to genetic engineering and provide a number of reasons for their opposition, some rooted in science, some sociocultural. But even here, the presentation of Zobrist and his ideas is mixed. Genetic engineering, as Sinskey makes clear, is less a sharp break with past scientific activity than a "clear next step," as one of the contributors to the Transhumanist

magazine *H+* put it. Such innovation "epitomize[s] the true potential of our species" (p. 294).

Brown has woven these ruminations throughout the novel,
mostly in characters' recollections of Zobrist. They set the stage
for a more direct exchange as the novel ends. The novel's many
chase scenes finally come to a halt in Istanbul, when Sienna,
after seizing a boat and eluding Langdon, returns to shore. She
explains the action of the virus released by Zobrist, which re-
sets the terms of the debate yet again. But, as we have seen at
each staging of the debate, no satisfactory resolution emerges.
Zobrist has not, as readers have been led to believe through the
entire novel, released a deadly genetic pestilence. He achieves
his goals by rendering a third of the population infertile, which,
by his calculations, will result in right-sizing the earth's population at a sustainable 4 billion. Now we are purely in the realm
of means, not ends, as Sienna and Langdon debate Zobrist's
response to the situation. Langdon labels Zobrist's act "genetic terrorism," plain and simple. Sienna, in opposing Zobrist's
plans, takes a more nuanced and troubled stance. She fears further, and more clearly evil, interventions, in which governments
or politically motivated groups would turn Zobrist's technology into a weapon. This puts Langdon into an awkward position, in which he defends the technology as a "godsend" (p.
440) a way to better life on a global scale.

It's worth stepping back a moment here to see what Brown
has done. He's opened a messy discussion, one in which people
can agree on fundamental points yet feel, as Langdon did when
he understood the consequences of Zobrist's alteration of the
genome, "ungrounded." And this prepares for the climax of
the novel, in which Sinskey, astonishingly, seems to acquiesce in
Zobrist's solution. Unlike Langdon, she makes no reference to
genetic terrorism; she makes a calculation of possible benefits.
Pragmatism seems to trump the abstractions of morality.

Let's recap. Zobrist's relation to Dante's poem is clear. He prizes it for its prophetic stance, its forthright and caustic view of the human condition and human weakness in confronting it. The form of Dante's journey also appeals to Zobrist—that redemption is achieved, paradoxically, by moving away from the Promised Land. And finally, Zobrist esteems the poem for its productivity. Writers have fitted the *Divine Comedy* to a number of situations over the poem's history, and Zobrist takes up that tradition boldly. He speaks through Dante's poem.

## "WHERE UP BECOMES DOWN"

Zobrist's Dantesque imagination, as we've seen, becomes a powerful and rich way of knowing the world. His response to the situation, of course, is questionable, but the novel certainly endorses his estimation of the depth of the crisis. Even Sinskey, at last, changes course and accepts Sienna's evaluation of Zobrist: "that he loved humankind, and that he simply longed so deeply to save our species that he was able to rationalize taking such drastic measures" (p. 454). Sinskey's departure for WHO headquarters, with the Transhumanist Sienna in tow, suggests that Zobrist's performance has raised her consciousness—as it was, after all, intended to do.

Sinskey's reversal is startling, and it asks us to reconsider many of the novel's events. Langdon, as one might expect, clarifies the book's attitude toward reversal. However ineffectual and belated his actions appear during the last quarter of the novel, his comments are quite suggestive, and they help us to understand Brown's relation to Dante. Let's look at two passages in the last gasping moments of the chase.

The first appears as Langdon approaches Hagia Sophia in Chapter 85. Langdon is troubled by Zobrist's use of Dante in the passage written on the back of the death mask:

the final canto of Dante's *Inferno* ended in a nearly identical scene: After a long descent through the underworld, Dante and Virgil reach the lowest point of hell. Here, with no way out, they hear the sounds of trickling water running through the stones beneath them, and they follow the rivulet though cracks and crevices . . . ultimately finding safety.

Dante wrote: *"A place is there below . . . which not by sight is known, but by the sound of a rivulet, which descends along the hollow of a rock . . . and by that hidden way, my guide and I did enter, to return to the fair world."*

Dante's scene had clearly been the inspiration for Zobrist's poem, although in this case, it seemed as if Zobrist had flipped everything upside down. Langdon and the others would indeed be following the sounds of trickling water, but unlike Dante, they would not be heading away from the inferno . . . but directly *into* it. (pp. 381–382)

We might note the prominence of reversal here, but if we consider the passage from the perspective we gain at the end of the novel, we might also note how it becomes a comment not only on the structure of Dante's poem but on Brown's plot, which turns upon surprise and reversal.

Let's recall the passage in Dante at question. The last canto of the *Inferno* concludes with an arduous and confusing climb, first down the body and flanks of Satan and then upward toward the southern hemisphere. Dante makes much of the mechanics of this passage. At a certain point, presumably the center of the Earth, he notes that Virgil "brought round his head to where his shanks had been and grappled on the hair like one who is climbing" (*Inf.* 34.79–80). Dante is flummoxed; Virgil painstakingly explains the shift in gravity that makes descent into ascent. (See figure 11 for a graphic representation of the reversal.) The canto ends with a lovely reminder of the providential nature of the journey, as Dante emerges to see, again,

Fig. 11.   Cornelis Galle, *Lucifer,* Courtesy of Albert and Shirley Small Special Collections Library, University of Virginia. This image shows Dante and Virgil climbing down Satan's body and the demarcation between the northern and southern hemispheres.

the stars. As he ascends, he hears the sound of water—water that flows, unlike the infernal ice of Cocytus, and water that is sign of God's grace. Both light and sound combine to make this one of the most beautiful moments in the poem.

This reversal in Dante's poem continues to haunt Langdon as he follows Zobrist's clues. Later, in Chapter 91, at what appears to be the climax of the novel—which we learn is completely anticlimactic—Langdon again recalls *Inferno* 34. As his hero approaches "ground zero," Brown releases a cascade of Dantesque references. Langdon descends into the cistern recalling various lines from the *Inferno* only to hear the strains of a concert provided by Zobrist, Liszt's *Dante Symphony*. As he nears the bag that contained the virus, he hears the chorus singing "Lasciate ogni speranza," the warning written on the Gate of Hell in Dante's poem. As he reaches the spot, Brown invokes canto 34 even more strongly, thinking, "Dante's *Inferno*. The finale. The center of the earth. Where gravity inverts itself. Where up becomes down" (p. 409). These references to Dante do much to heighten the suspense of the situation, but it's hard not to read further into them. Reversal, typified by the utterly stupefying inversion Dante experiences in *Inferno* 34, provides a conceptual model for the novel. The way down is the way up. Zobrist is first villain, then harbinger of global crisis.

From the perspective of the final chapter, one can see how deep this structure of reversal runs in the novel. Nothing is really as it seemed. Sienna is first friend, then foe, and finally ally. Sinskey is at once hostage, relentless tormentor, and cautious supporter of Zobrist. Bruder menaces then helps Langdon. Vayentha's lethal gunshots are blanks. And Langdon's frenetic efforts to head off the release of the virus are belated and spectacularly useless. In fact, the entire plot of the novel is Zobrist's invention—the hunted turns out to be leading the hunters. And these plot twists simply parallel what seems to be Brown's point about overpopulation—that our recognition of the crisis, long delayed by denial, can be as instantaneous a reversal as that experienced by Dante in *Inferno* 34. What, we can now say, could be more fitting a symbol for Zobrist's plot than the inverted head of the Medusa that marks the spot of "ground zero"? If Zobrist takes up Dante's poem as a vehicle for prophecy, then Brown seems to take up Dante's poem as a pattern for his plot and his exercise in consciousness raising. In each case, a part of the *Divine Comedy*'s legacy is emphasized and activated. Both Brown and his creation Zobrist take part in the Dantesque tradition.

## TRADITIONS AND READERS

Dan Brown's novels are often criticized for wooden dialogue, clumsy transitions, and undeveloped characters. One might even dismiss them as a kind of mash-up, in which the author takes ready-made scenarios from popular culture and concatenates them. It's not hard to trace such ready-made material: The Zobrist character incorporates the "evil villain" from any number of Bond films; Vayentha, at first glance, recalls Lisbeth Salander, the transgressive heroine from Stieg Larsson's trilogy; the provost's rule-bound musings recall the meditations of Jason Statham in *The Transporter* (2002); Langdon's attempts to retrace actions he has forgotten call to mind the protagonist of Christopher Nolan's *Memento* (2000). The idea of a global pandemic has been used in films like *Outbreak* (1995), *Contagion* (2011), and, thinking back a bit further, *The Andromeda Strain* (1971). Nor is the idea of an adventurous professor unfamiliar to audiences after Indiana Jones's appearance in *Raiders of the Lost Ark* (1981) and three sequels.

These strictures are true but somewhat beside the point. The real problem in his work is a failure to fuse various elements of his fiction. Parts seem extraneous or digressive. An obvious example of this weakness is Langdon's tiresome performances as tour guide. Even during the most frantic of chases, he pauses to inform us about some statue or building—often in the most irrelevant of terms, such as giving its height—as if he were a docent moving through a museum trailed by an overtaxed group of tourists.

But Brown's *Inferno* does begin to move toward the integration of elements. If the core of the novel concerns denial and inversion—the avoidance of the population crisis and the swift transformations of perspective that the characters experience— then we can see how certain subplots in the novel contribute to these larger structures. The Consortium, with its rule-bound provost, is important to moving the plot along, providing a for- midable adversary for both Sinskey and Langdon. But viewed from the larger thematic perspective, the Consortium becomes a study in how denial is maintained by powerful groups and individuals who purchase the Consortium's services.

We don't argue that Brown's *Inferno* is great literature in the way that a book like Charles Dickens' *Great Expectations* or F. Scott Fitzgerald's *Great Gatsby* is. But we do think that books should be evaluated, at least partly, on their own terms, or in terms of what they do well. Moreover, a book's greatness lies not only in the book itself: For books to become great— that is, to enter a live tradition of literature—great readers are required, audiences who coalesce around a work and, through their own active imaginations, extend it. If Brown's *Inferno*, as the author himself has hoped it might, turns readers back toward Dante's masterpiece with renewed interest and appre- ciation, then this is no small achievement.

# 9

# A Complete List of Allusions to the Divine Comedy in Dan Brown's Inferno *

In the last chapter we saw some of the ways in which Dan Brown adapts Dante's *Divine Comedy*. But there are also many other notions he picks up from Dante.

---

* For all page numbers in Dan Brown's *Inferno* we used: Dan Brown, *The Inferno* (New York: Doubleday), 2013.

We've assembled a complete list of Brown's allusions to facilitate readers' own explorations. This list is intended to help
readers pursue their inquiries into Dan Brown's use of Dante.

In this section we note references to the *Divine Comedy*
in Dan Brown's *Inferno,* organized by page number. We reproduce the mention in the novel as a paraphrase or an extract,
then point out and discuss the exact passage in Dante's poem to
which the references allude.

## PAGE 1, EPIGRAPH

> The darkest places in hell are reserved for those who main-
> tain their neutrality in times of moral crisis.

Here Brown refers to Dante's punishment of the neutrals (*Inf.*
3.34–63). Just inside the Gate of Hell, Dante sees "the sorry
souls of those who lived without infamy and without praise."
Generally referred to as the neutrals or pusillanimous, these are
weak-minded souls who never took a position in life. They are
the first damned souls Dante sees. However, they are not among
the "blackest" souls in Hell. The glutton Ciacco uses this expression (*Inf.* 6. 85) when Dante asks him the whereabouts of some
historical Italians, among them Farinata, Tegghiaio, Mosca, and
Jacopo Rusticucci, all of whom Dante encounters in Lower Hell.

## PAGE 3, FACT

> *Inferno* is the underworld as described in Dante Alighieri's
> epic poem *The Divine Comedy,* which portrays hell as an
> elaborately structured realm populated by entities known as
> "shades"—bodiless souls trapped between life and death.

Dante uses the terms "shades" and "souls" to describe those
he meets in the Afterlife. As he makes his way across the circle

of the gluttons who wallow while pelted relentlessly by filthy precipitation, Dante walks on "their empty images that seemed like persons" (*Inf.* 6.36). The bodies of the souls in Hell have no substance. However, there are moments, especially in Lower Hell, where they seem corporeal: the sowers of discord spew blood everywhere (*Inf.* 28); Dante kicks the head and pulls the hair of the traitor Bocca degli Abati (*Inf.* 32.75–105). In such instances Dante employs poetic license.

### PAGE 5, PROLOGUE

> *Through the dolent city, I flee.*
> *Through the eternal woe, I take flight*

The Shade utters these words at the beginning of the novel. The phrase "dolent city" is an old-fashioned translation of "*città dolente,*" part of the inscription over the Gate of Hell (*Inf.* 3.1). Charles Singleton translates the phrase as "woeful city." Throughout the *Inferno*, Dante uses a number circumlocutions or roundabout expressions to refer to Hell: "eternal place" (*Inf.* 1.114), "this blind prison" (*Inf.* 10.59), "the deep foul valley" (*Inf.* 12.40). The wording differs depending on the translation. These expressions enhance Dante's characterization of Hell.

Readers can find all the expressions Dante uses to refer to Hell on the World of Dante Web site (www.worldofdante.org). On the home page go to Search, then Place, type "Inferno" in the Name box, then hit the Places button.

> Along the banks of the river Arno, I scramble, breathless . . .

A few paragraphs later, Brown mentions some places in Florence—Piazza San Firenze, Bargello, and the Badia. Dante mentions the Arno four times in cantos 13, 23, 30, and 33. He also mentions monuments of Florence such as the Baptistery (*Inf.* 19) and the Ponte Vecchio (*Inf.* 13).

Here all hesitation must be left behind.

Right after Dante reads the inscription on the Gate of Hell, Virgil tells him "Here must all fear be left behind; here let all cowardice be dead" (*Inf.* 3.14.15).

Ungrateful land!

When Dante asks Ciacco the glutton about the causes of division in Florence, he cites the envy, pride, and avariciousness of Florentines (*Inf.* 6.75). Brunetto Latini, one of the Florentine sodomites, characterizes Florentines as "a people avaricious, envious and proud" (*Inf.* 15.67–68).

## PAGES 5–6

. . . the lustful bodies writhing in fiery rain, the gluttonous souls floating in excrement . . .

The lustful are pummeled by a hellish hurricane (*Inf.* 5.31–33). The gluttons wallow in filthy mud and are pelted by all manner of filthy precipitation (*Inf.* 6.7–12). A rain of fire pours down on the blasphemers, sodomites, and usurers (*Inf.* 14.28–29). The Shade, Bertrand Zobrist, has confused the punishment of the lustful and gluttons.

## PAGE 6

Far below is the blessed city that I have made my sanctuary from those who exiled me.

There are a number of references to Dante's exile in the *Inferno*. Brunetto Latini and Farinata make two of the most explicit references (*Inf.* 10.76–81and *Inf.* 15.61–78 respectively.) See chapter 3 for a discussion of these allusions.

> Guide me, dear Virgil, across the void.

Dante's guide through Hell and Purgatory is the Roman poet Virgil. We discuss Dante's choice of guides in chapter 1.

## PAGE 7

> . . . simmering beneath the bloodred waters of the lagoon that reflects no stars.

Those who were violent against others (murderers, plunderers, tyrants) boil in the Phlegethon, one of the rivers of Hell in the classical Hades. Dante's Phlegethon is a "river of blood . . . in which boils everyone who by violence injures others" (*Inf.* 12.47–48). "Stars" are an important reference for Dante. He concludes each canticle in the *Divine Comedy* with a mention of them.

## PAGE 9

> Robert Langdon gazed at her across a river whose churning waters ran red with blood.

In *Purgatory,* Dante sees Matelda, who presides over the Earthly Paradise, across the river Lethe (*Purg.* 28.37–75). See also the note for Page 7 on this list.

Langdon sees hundreds of bodies in the river,

> consumed by fire, buried in feces, devouring one another.

The heretics are confined in burning tombs (*Inf.* 10), the flatterers are immersed in excrement (*Inf.* 18), and, among the traitors, Ugolino gnaws on the head of Archbishop Ruggieri (*Inf.* 32 and 33). Satan also feasts on Judas, Brutus, and Cassius (*Inf.* 34). Langdon saw these details on Botticelli's Map of Hell. The actual map is quite small, as are its online versions. To view details, go to the Maps link on the World of Dante site. The first map is Botticelli's Map of Hell: You can enlarge it and view an interactive version to see every circle and region of Hell labeled.

## PAGES 9–10

The veiled woman (Dr. Sinskey) across the river points to a

> writhing pair of legs, which protruded upside down from the earth, apparently belonging to some poor soul who had been buried headfirst to his waist.

The simonists are buried upside-down in holes in the bedrock of Hell. Fire burns the soles of their feet. We discuss the punishment of simonist popes in chapter 4. You can also see them on Botticelli's Map of Hell.

## PAGE 29

Langdon recalls again the veiled woman:

> on the banks of a bloodred river and surrounded by writhing bodies. . . . [Their] half-buried, upside-down legs were falling limp . . .

For the bloodred river, see the note to page 7. The wrathful writhe in the swamp of Styx. They are described in *Inf.*

7.100–126 and *Inf.* 8.31–63. For the upside-down legs, see the note to pages 9–10.


PAGE 29

Another reference to the silver-haired woman (Dr. Sinskey) across a bloodred river.

References to the shouts of desperation, putrid air, and sounds of tortured souls thrashing in agony recall Dante's first impressions upon entering Hell, where he hears horrible sounds of suffering (*Inf.* 3.22–30). For the bloodred river, see the note to page 7.


PAGE 58

The seal on the canister containing an image of Botticelli's Map of Hell

> bore an especially gruesome carving—a three-headed, horned Satan who was in the process of eating three different men at once, one man in each of his three mouths.

> Langdon talks about Satan as

> an icon associated with the Black Death. (58)

Dante does not associate Satan with the Black Death. Dante's Satan feasts on the souls of Brutus, Cassius, and Judas (*Inf.* 34.55–67). Each face is a different color: dirty white, red, and black. Cassius is in the dirty white mouth, Judas the red one, and Brutus, the black. The three are traitors to benefactors: Brutus and Cassius betrayed Caesar; Judas betrayed Christ.

PAGE 64

Langdon offers general information on the *Divine Comedy*—
its division into three canticles, its author, the popularity of
*Inferno*. He mentions the punishment of the lustful ("blown
about by an eternal windstorm"), the gluttons ("forced to lie
face down in a vile slush of sewage"), and heretics ("trapped in
flaming coffins").

The description of the punishments of the lustful and gluttons
is accurate. However, gluttons are also assailed by Cerberus's
incessant howling and pelted relentlessly by filthy precipitation.
See Dante's *Inferno* 5 (lustful), 6 (gluttons), and 10 (heretics).
We discuss Dante's treatment of the lustful and gluttons in
chapter 2 and the heretics in chapter 3.

PAGES 64–65

> In the seven centuries since its publication, Dante's enduring
> vision of hell had inspired tributes, translations, and varia-
> tions by some of history's greatest creative minds.

See chapters 7 and 8 for a discussion of classic and popular
adaptations of Dante's *Inferno*.

PAGE 66

Langdon mentions the punishments of three groups of sinners
in Malebolge: The seducers are whipped by demons, the thieves
are bitten by snakes, and corrupt politicians boil in tar.

Malebolge forms the eighth circle of Hell. Here Dante visits
the fraudulent. Malebolge is divided into ten sections, each of
which is commonly referred to as a ditch or pouch. In *Inferno*
11, Virgil provides an overview of the sins punished in Hell. He

mentions the sins of fraud in lines 52 to 60. In *Inf.* 18.1–15, Dante provides an overview of the topography of the eighth circle, which he compares to a pit.

Dante's punishment of the thieves is far more complex than what Langdon describes. The thieves are punished in different ways: They are attacked and bound by snakes and other reptilian creatures, bitten, incinerated and resurrected in a lightning-fast process. There are also other punishments: At times the thieves fuse with the snakes and are transformed into one hybrid monster; other times they exchange natures with the reptilian beasts in a reciprocal process of metamorphosis. We discuss these striking transformations in chapter 1.

PAGE 75

Zobrist gives the provost a gift (the canister that projects Botticelli's Map of Hell) for Dr. Sinskey and calls it

" . . . her own personal Virgil . . ."

Virgil is Dante's guide through Hell and most of Purgatory. See *Inferno* 1 for Dante's account of their initial meeting.

PAGE 77

The provost looks at the first page of the *Divine Comedy* that Zobrist has given him. He reads the opening tercet of *Inferno* 1 and sees an inscription from Zobrist thanking him for

helping me find the path.

In *Inf.* 1.3, Dante refers to having lost "the straight way" (Singleton's translation) or the "straightforward path" (translation used by Dan Brown). The "straight way" is the proverbial "straight and narrow."

PAGE 80

Langdon mentions Dante's close ties to Florence and the bitterness of his exile from his beloved native city, citing lines from the poem:

> You shall leave everything you love most . . . This is the arrow that the bow of exile shoots first.

Here Langdon quotes Cacciaguida, Dante's great-great-grandfather, whom the pilgrim encounters in the Heaven of Jupiter in *Paradise* 15–17 (the lines are from *Par.* 17.55–57). Throughout his journey, Dante has heard a number of references to his exile. Farinata (*Inf.* 10) and Brunetto Latini (*Inf.* 15) are among the souls who allude to it directly. These earlier allusions, however, are cast in the riddle-like language of prophecies. Cacciaguida decodes these earlier prophecies and speaks directly about the pains of exile. We discuss Dante's love-hate relationship to Florence in chapter 5.

> *The river,* Langdon thought with a touch of trepidation. Dante's famous journey into hell had begun by crossing a river as well.

Dante sees the recently damned souls gathered on one shore of the river Acheron in *Inferno* 3. Charon, ferryman of the dead, transports the damned across the river but tells Dante that "By another way, by other ports, not here, you shall cross to shore. A lighter bark must carry you" (*Inf.* 3.91–93). A sudden whirlwind bursts through the scene and red light flashes, causing the pilgrim to faint. When he awakens, he finds himself on the other side of the Acheron. No explanation is offered on how Dante is transported to the other side.

PAGE 82

Langdon defines tragedy and comedy, noting that

> Tragedy, representing high literature, was written in formal Italian; comedy, representing low literature, was written in the vernacular and geared toward the general population.

There are a number of inaccuracies in this explanation. The Italian language was in a state of flux in Dante's time and had not been "formalized." Whether one speaks of "formal Italian" or the vernacular, both refer to works written in Italian. Epics like Virgil's *Aeneid* were written in Latin in a lofty style. Dante uses the word "*comedìa*" ("comedy") for the first time in *Inf.* 16.128 as he swears that he saw the figure of Geryon, the monster that presides over the eighth circle (of fraud), rising up to him from an abyss. The adjective "divine" was added to a 1555 edition of the poem, and by the eighteenth century, editors and scholars frequently referred to the poem by the title *Divine Comedy.*

The word "comedy" had a specific meaning in Dante's time, somewhat different from its meaning for us. It referred to a work written in a mixed style, a combination of high and low, that began unhappily but ended well. Dante employs a range of stylistic registers in the poem. He uses regional dialectal words, the lofty tone we associate with epics like Virgil's *Aeneid,* colloquial expressions, and, at times, very crude expressions, all of which lend expressive force and variety to his poem.

PAGE 83

Langdon refers to the way in which Dante's *Inferno* inspired details in Michelangelo's *Last Judgment,* notably the depiction of Charon.

Dante describes Charon's fiery orbs in *Inferno* 3.109: His eyes burn "like glowing coals."

PAGE 100

Zobrist shows Elizabeth Sinskey Gustave Doré's illustration of

> a vast sea of humanity, throngs of sickly people . . .

The falsifiers are punished in the last ditch of Malebolge: All suffer from a debilitating disease. Falsifiers of metals, or alchemists, suffer from leprosy. Falsifiers of people, or impersonators, suffer from something like hydrophobia. Falsifiers of money, or counterfeiters, suffer from dropsy. Falsifiers of words, or liars, suffer from a raging fever. Dante's moral objection to the falsifiers' behavior is connected to his condemnation of fraud in general. Perversion of the good and real things in the world (metals, words, currency, persons) toward deceitful ends is an offense against central principles of divine order and justice in the world. Doré's illustration can be viewed on the World of Dante site: go to the Gallery link, then Doré. However, Doré's illustrations for *Inf.* 29.55 and *Inf.* 29.82 do not depict a "vast sea of humanity."

PAGE 103

When he confronts Dr. Sinskey, Zobrist refers to

> Dante's deadly sins—greed, gluttony, treachery, murder, and
> the rest . . .

The seven deadly sins include pride, envy, avarice, wrath, sloth, gluttony, and lust. Treachery and murder are not among the deadly sins, although they are among the sins punished in

Dante's *Inferno*. Although some of the sins punished in *Inferno* (lust, gluttony, avarice, and wrath) are among the seven deadly sins, others such as treachery and murder derive from Ciceronian and Aristotelian juridical texts. See Virgil's explanation of the "plan of Hell" in *Inferno* 11. A good commentary to the poem, such as those of Charles Singleton or Robert Hollander, would provide a fuller account.

## PAGE 142

While crossing the Ponte Vecchio in Florence with Sienna Brooks, Langdon refers to the murder of a Florentine nobleman, Buondelmonte, in 1216.

Dante and many of his contemporaries consider the murder of Buondelmonte the event that initiated the division between the Guelfs and the Ghibellines. See chapter 3 for a discussion of this event and the Guelf-Ghibelline split. Dante refers to Buondelmonte's murder in *Par.* 16.136–147.

## PAGE 155

While in the Palazzo Vecchio with Sienna Brooks, Langdon, thinking of the phrase "the eyes of death," recalls:

> Skulls were a recurring theme in Dante's *Inferno*, most famously Count Ugolino's brutal punishment . . . that of being sentenced to gnaw on the skull of the wicked archbishop. (155)

Dante encounters Ugolino among the traitors to one's party or homeland in the ninth circle. Traitors are frozen in the lake of Cocytus. Ugolino and Archbishop Ruggieri are imprisoned in the same hole. When Dante comes across the two, he sees the grisly meal Ugolino makes of the archbishop's brains. We discuss Ugolino's punishment in chapter 5. Skulls are not a recurring theme in the *Inferno*.

## PAGE 163

Zobrist leaves a message for Dr. Sinskey, essentially the same message as the novel's epigraph:

> *The darkest places in hell*
> *are reserved for those*
> *who maintain their neutrality*
> *in times of moral crisis.*

See the note to Page 1.

## PAGE 166

Marta Alvarez, a cultural administrator at the Palazzo Vecchio, speculates that the sad expression on Dante's death mask is related to his love for Beatrice.

In an earlier work, the *Vita Nuova* (*New Life*), Dante details aspects of his love for Beatrice in a series of poems and prose commentaries.

## PAGE 195

While trying to escape the Palazzo Vecchio, Langdon and Sienna go through a secret passageway behind the map of Armenia in the Hall of Geographical Maps. Langdon refers to "Satan's navel" and notes that

> Sometimes you need to go up . . . to go down.

Sienna remembers this dramatic passage from *Inf.* 34.76–111.

After pointing out the last of the sinners, Virgil informs Dante that they have now seen everything and that they must now exit Hell (*Inf.* 34.69). The two wayfarers must climb down Satan's body: His trunk is in the northern hemisphere, the legs in the southern one. Satan's groin occupies the dead center of Earth. In line 79, Virgil passes the center of Earth and makes a 180-degree turn. Virgil chooses the propitious moment, when Satan's wings are open (line 72), and spies an open area from which he and Dante begin their downward climb. Virgil starts feet first down the body and then turns to climb up. With Dante on his back, he turns himself upside-down, in order to proceed head first at the point where Satan's thigh joins his hip. Dante and his contemporaries believed that the force of gravity was greater at the center of Earth, hence the difficulty of Virgil's climb.

In line 85 we see Dante and Virgil slipping through a chink between Satan's thigh and the bottom of the ice. They emerge into a cavern that is situated on the other side of Earth's center. Dante does not realize that they have crossed into the southern hemisphere. When he looks back into Hell, Satan appears upside-down, and Dante thinks they are going back into Hell.

PAGE 215

Langdon tells Sienna that Dante

denounce[s] pride as the *worst* of the seven deadly sins . . .
and punished the prideful in the deepest ring of the inferno.

While Dante considers pride the worst of the sins in Purgatory, the lowest ring of Hell is reserved for traitors.

PAGES 228–229

Inside the Church of Santa Maria dei Cerchi, Langdon borrows a visitor's iPhone to check the text of *Paradise* 25. The first two tercets are cited.

In these lines Dante imagines a happy return to Florence, where he would put on the laurel crown, that is, be honored publicly for his work. He hopes that his "sacred poem," the *Divine Comedy*, will overcome the cruelty of his enemies (Black Guelfs) and that this crowning will take place at the baptismal font in the baptistery of San Giovanni. He refers to Florence in the same passage as the "fair sheepfold."

Dante also refers to the San Giovanni baptismal font in *Inf*. 19.16–18 to give readers a sense of the size of the holes in which the simonists are inserted upside-down.

PAGE 231

Langdon recalls the first lines from *Paradise* 25 again.

See the note to page 215.

PAGE 239

Langdon and Sienna gaze at the mosaic of Satan in Florence's baptistery. Langdon recalls that Dante's Satan, who feasts on three sinners, was likely inspired by this image and refers to lines *Inf*.34.28 in which Dante refers to Satan as "the emperor of the despondent kingdom."

This is one of the roundabout phrases that Dante uses in this canto to refer to Satan. Others include "the creature who was once so fair" (line 18) and "the evil worm that pierces the world" (line 108). Readers can search for all expressions Dante uses to refer to Satan on the Search page of the World of Dante: go to Creatures, type Satan, then hit the search Creatures button. See also the note for page 58.

## PAGE 241

Langdon informs Sienna that

> allegedly Dante once jumped into the font to save a drowning child.

Dante mentions this incident in *Inf.* 19.19–21. This autobiographical reference is something of a mystery since no other record of it exists. Given that the fonts were made of marble, it is difficult to imagine how Dante "broke" it.

## PAGES 247–248

Langdon and Sienna, now in possession of the Dante death mask, see seven "P's" written across the forehead of the mask. Langdon explains that the letters all refer to the same word, *peccatum,* Latin for "sin."

Upon entering the gate to Purgatory proper, an angel inscribes seven "P's" on Dante's forehead. After he visits each terrace, each of which houses souls purging themselves of one of the seven deadly sins, an angel erases one of the "P's." The process is explained in *Purg.* 9.112–114.

## PAGE 253

While examining the writing in the Dante mask, Langdon and Sienna see this phrase

> O you possessed of sturdy intellect

Langdon notes:

> It's taken from one of the most famous stanzas [sic] of
> Dante's *Inferno*.

Dante the poet addresses the reader directly in these lines, asking us to "mark the doctrine that is hidden under the veil of
the strange verses" (*Inf.* 9.62–63). This is a highly symbolic
moment in the poem as Dante and Virgil are about to enter
Lower Hell. Those "who have sound understanding"—that is,
invested with the capability of discerning the truth—should ob-
serve the teaching, the allegory that underlies these verses. The
"teaching" alludes to the deeper truth or message concealed
within the symbolism of the narrative at this point, namely that
while powers such as Virgil's are inadequate, God always gives
his grace to help the good against the forces of evil. The distinction partly emphasizes the difference between Virgil's reason
and a Christian's divinely inspired mind.

## PAGE 276

In thinking who might be the "treacherous doge," Langdon
notes:

> "Treachery is one of the Seven Deadly Sins . . ."

The seven deadly sins are pride, envy, avarice, wrath, sloth,
gluttony, and lust. Treachery is not one of these sins, although
Dante's ninth circle of Hell houses the traitors. See also the note
to page 103.

PAGE 280

Langdon notes that

> in the finale of the *Inferno,* we find Dante listening to the
> sound of trickling water inside a chasm and following it
> through an opening . . . which leads him out of hell.

In *Inf.* 34.127–132, we see Dante exit Hell to the sound of the
rushing of a stream. Since the cavern is dark, the sound of the
stream helps to orient the two travelers. The stream comes from
the river Lethe in the Earthly Paradise.

PAGE 300

Langdon notes that St. Lucia (St. Lucy) is one of the

> three blessed women . . . who helped summon Virgil to help
> Dante escape the underworld.

St. Lucy is one of the three women, along with the Virgin Mary
and Beatrice, who take pity on Dante's plight in the Dark Wood.
Mary calls to Lucy who then summons Beatrice. However, it is
Beatrice alone who visits Virgil in Limbo to seek his assistance.
See *Inf.* 2.94–105, 124.

PAGE 305

Langdon notes that Dante had seen the repairing of ships in the
Venetian Arsenal and that this inspired the punishment of the
barrators, corrupt politicians, who boil in tar.

Dante compares the hubbub of activity among the barrators
and the demons that patrol this ditch of Malebolge to the range

of activity that takes place in the Venetian Arsenal during winter months when ships are repaired with tar. See *Inf.* 21.7–18.

### PAGE 320

Zobrist compares his love for Sienna to Dante's love for Beatrice, wishing that he could hold his flaming heart before her as Dante held his before Beatrice.

Zobrist's recollection is imprecise. This scene evokes the third chapter of the *Vita Nuova* in which the God of Love holds Beatrice swathed in a red cloth and places Dante's flaming heart before her, imploring her to eat it.

### PAGE 381–2

Pondering again the inscription Zobrist has written inside Dante's death mask, Langdon, now in Istanbul, recalls again sound of the rivulet that Dante and Virgil hear as they make the ascent through the underground cavern beneath the southern hemisphere.

See the note to page 253.

### PAGE 405

Langdon listens to the chorus singing to Liszt's *Dante Symphony* and hears the chant

> Abandon all hope, ye who enter here!

These are the last words inscribed over the Gate of Hell (*Inf.* 3.9).

PAGE 407

In a cavern below Istanbul's cistern, Langdon recalls the first two lines from the first canto of the *Inferno*.

In these lines, Dante the pilgrim describes himself as being in a dark wood having lost the path that does not stray. Langdon refers to this as the "straightforward pathway." See the note to page 77 and to pages 9 and 9–10, in which we discuss the opening lines of the poem.

PAGE 409

Langdon recalls a detail from *Inferno* 34 again:

> The finale. The center of the earth. Where gravity inverts itself. Where up becomes down.

See the note to page 195.

PAGE 457

Langdon recalls an ancient saying, noting that some attribute this to Dante himself:

> Remember tonight . . . for it's the beginning of forever.

This phrase, while often attributed to Dante, does not appear in his poetry.

PAGE 463, EPILOGUE

Last sentence of Brown's novel:

The sky had become a glistening tapestry of stars.

Brown clearly echoes Dante, who ends each canticle of the poem with the beautiful word "*stelle*" (stars).

# APPENDIX

# Timeline of Dante's Times and Life

**Bold items refer to Dante's life.**

| | |
|---|---|
| 1210 | Innocent III approves the Regula primitiva (primitive rule) of the Franciscan Order by St. Francis. |
| 1215 | Murder of Buondelmonte de' Buondelmonti (*Inf.* 28. 103–11; *Par.* 16.140–41). |
| 1216 | 22 December: Honorius III approves Ordo Praedicatorum (Order of Preachers), the Dominican Order. |
| 1223 | Honorius III approves the Regula bullata (the Second Rule) of the Franciscan Order (*Par.* 11.97–99). |
| 1228–1252 | First church of Santa Croce (Franciscan basilica of Florence) constructed. Building of the current structure begins in 1294. |
| 1246 | (ca.) Birth of Dino Compagni, chronicler of Florence (d. 1324). |
| 1246–1360 | (ca.) Construction of Santa Maria Novella, Dominican church of Florence. |
| 1248 | Ghibelline force led by the Uberti drive Guelfs out of Florence (*Inf.* 10.48). |
| 1250 | Guelfs receive permission to return to Florence (*Inf.* 10.49). |

|  | Beginning of the first popular government (Primo Popolo). |
|---|---|
|  | 13 December: Death of Frederick II. |
| 1252 | Gold florin minted in Florence. |
| 1253–1260 | Brunetto Latini is chancellor of the Primo Popolo. |
| 1257–1273 | St. Bonaventure is minister general of the Franciscan Order. |
| 1258 | Ghibellines flee after their conspiracy to break up popular government is discovered. |
| 1259–1260 | Nicola Pisano sculpts the pulpit of Baptistry in Pisa. |
| 1260 | End of the Primo Popolo government. |
|  | 4 September: Battle of Montaperti (*Inf.* 10.85–87; *Inf.* 32.76–123). Exiled Sienese and Florentine Ghibellines, led by Farinata degli Uberti, defeat Florentine Guelfs. Defeated Guelfs seek refuge in Lucca. |
| 1260–1267 | Ghibellines in control of Florence. |
| 1261 | Election of Urban IV as pope. |
|  | Establishment of Frati Gaudenti (Jolly Friars) in Bologna. |
| 1263 | St. Bonaventure, *Legenda Maior Sancti Francisci* (biography of St. Francis). |
| 1264 | Death of Urban IV. |
|  | Death of Farinata degli Uberti. |
| 1265 | **Late May–Early June: Birth of Dante in the San Martino quarter of Florence.** |
|  | Election of Clement IV as pope. |
| 1265–1268 | Nicola Pisano sculpts the pulpit of Baptistry in Siena. |
| 1266 | (ca.) Birth of Giotto, painter. |
|  | 6 January: Charles I of Anjou crowned King of Sicily. |
|  | 26 February: Charles I of Anjou defeats and kills Manfred and the Ghibellines at the Battle of Benevento (*Purg.* 3.103–143). |
| 1266–1267 | Brief revival of popular movement followed by return of Guelfs to power after Battle of Benevento. |
| 1268 | Death of Clement IV. |
|  | 23 August: Charles I of Anjou defeats Frederick II's grandson Conradin at Battle of Tagliacozzo. |
| 1269 | June: Battle of Colle val d'Elsa: Florentine Guelfs, led by Aldobrandino de'Pazzi and Jean Britaud (Charles I of |

Anjou's vicar), defeat Sienese Ghibellines led by Provenzan Salvani.

| | |
|---|---|
| 1270 | Bono Giamboni, *Libro de' vizi e delle virtudi* (Book of vices and virtues). |
| | Birth of Cino da Pistoia (d. 1327). |
| 1270–1275 | **Death of Dante's mother, Bella.** |
| 1271 | 13 March: Guy de Montfort murders Henry of Cornwall during mass at church of San Silvestro, Viterbo (*Inf.* 12.119–120). |
| | Election of Gregory X as pope. |
| 1273 | Election of Rudolph of Habsburg as Holy Roman Emperor. |
| 1274 | Second Council of Lyons (adoption of the doctrine of Purgatory). |
| | **May: First encounter with Beatrice.** |
| | Death of Thomas Aquinas. |
| | Death of Bonaventure. |
| 1276 | Death of Gregory X. |
| | Election of Innocent V as pope and death in same year. |
| | Election of Adrian V as pope and death in same year (*Purg.* 19.103–105). |
| | Election of John XXI as pope. |
| | (ca.) Death of Guido Guinizelli. |
| | (ca.) Birth of Giovanni Villani. |
| 1277 | **(ca.) Studies with local professional teachers.** |
| | Death of John XXI. |
| | 25 November: Election of Nicholas III as pope. |
| | **9 January: Marriage contract with Gemma Donati.** |
| 1279 | Nicholas III sends Cardinal Latino Malabranca to negotiate reconciliation between Guelfs and Ghibellines, resulting in short-lived bipartisan government. |
| 1280 | **Death of cousin Geri del Bello in brawl (*Inf.* 28–29).** |
| | Death of Nicholas III. |
| 1281 | Election of Martin IV as pope. |
| 1281–1283 | **Death of Dante's father, Alighiero Alighieri.** |

| 1282 | Rebellion of Sicilian Vespers (*Par.* 8.67–75): Peter of Aragon expels Angevins from Sicily. Division of Kingdom of Sicily into Naples (under Angevins) and Sicily (under Aragonese). |
| | June–August: Establishment of priorate, a guild-based rather than factional system of government; factions remain. |
| 1282–1283 | Paolo Malatesta, Captain of Commune of Florence. |
| 1283 | **Second recorded encounter with Beatrice; first poems; friendship with Guido Cavalcanti begins.** |
| 1284–1334 | Construction of third circuit of walls in Florence (second circuit of walls constructed in 1178). |
| 1285 | Death of Charles I of Anjou, King of Naples, and accession of Charles II to throne. |
| | Death of Philip III, King of France, and accession of Philip IV to the throne. |
| | Death of Martin IV and election of Honorius IV as pope. |
| | **(1285 or 1290) Marriage to Gemma Donati.** |
| | Duccio paints *Rucellai Madonna* for Santa Maria Novella. |
| 1285–1289 | Franciscan spiritual Ubertino da Casale at Santa Croce. |
| 1286 | Construction of hospital of Santa Maria Nuova begins. |
| 1286–1287 | **Summer 1286–early 1287: Resides in Bologna (date uncertain).** |
| 1287 | Death of Honorius IV. |
| | **(1287, 1290, or 1295) Birth of son Pietro.** |
| 1287–1289 | Franciscan spiritual Pietro di Giovanni Olivi teaches at Santa Croce. |
| 1287–1295 | Andrea de' Mozzi, Bishop of Florence (*Inf.* 15.112–114). |
| 1288 | Election of Nicholas IV as pope (first Franciscan pope). |
| | (ca.) Cimabue paints frescoes at upper church of San Francisco, Assisi. |
| 1288–1289 | Imprisonment of Ugolino della Gherardesca in Tower of Hunger in Pisa (*Inf.* 33.20–23). |
| 1289 | **June: Takes part in Battle of Campaldino: Blacks led by Corso Donati and Vieri de' Cerchi defeat Ghibellines of Arezzo led by Bonconte da Montefeltro (*Purg.* 5.85–129).** |
| 1290 | **16 August: Takes part in siege and seizure of fortress of Caprona (*Inf.* 21.94–96).** |

| | |
|---|---|
| 1290 | June: Death of Beatrice. |
| | July–November: Guido da Polenta the Elder, Podestà (mayoral-like position) of Florence. |
| | **(1290, 1292, or 1297) Birth of son Jacopo.** |
| 1291 | Death of Rudolph of Habsburg. |
| 1292 | **(1292 or 1294) Writes** *Vita Nuova*. |
| | Death of Nicholas IV. |
| 1293 | 18 January: Ordinances of Justice (series of reforms) introduced by priors in Florence. Office of *Gonfaloniere della Giustizia* (standard-bearer of Justice) introduced. |
| 1293–1294 | Death of Brunetto Latini. |
| | Death of Guittone d'Arezzo. |
| 1293–1295 | Giano della Bella leads revival of popular government, Secondo Popolo (*Par.* 16.131–32). |
| 1293–1296 | **(ca.) Exchanges tenzone with Forese Donati (*Purg.* 23. 76–77).** |
| 1294 | **Friendship with Charles Martel of Anjou (in Florence at the time), King of Hungary and heir to throne of Naples (*Par.* 8–9).** |
| | Election of Celestine V as pope and abdication in same year. |
| | Election of Boniface VIII as pope. |
| 1295 | **Beginning of political career among Trentasei del Capitano, 36 representatives of the "populace."** |
| | July–August: Enrolls in Guild of Physicians and Apothecaries (Arte dei Medici e Speziali) to qualify for political office (date uncertain). |
| | 6 July: Proposes modifications of Ordinamenti di Giustizia, ordinances against power of nobles in Florence. |
| 1295–1296 | November 1295–April 1296: Member of Council of Thirty-Six (Consiglio dei Trentasei del Capitano del Popolo). |
| | May–September: Member of Council of the Hundred (Consiglio dei Cento). |
| 1296 | July: Argues that Florence should not offer refuge to exiles of Pistoia and proposes that priors and Gonfaloniere di Giustizia should be empowered to initiate proceedings against anyone assaulting or insulting members of the *popolano*. |

December: Writes the four *petrose* poems.

1298    Construction of new palace of priors (now Palazzo Vecchio) begins.

September: Boniface VIII elicits advice from Guido da Montefeltro on how to capture Palestrina, fortified stronghold of Colonna family (*Inf.* 27.100–102).

(ca.) Marco Polo dictates account of travels to the Far East to Rustichello of Pisa.

1299    Birth of daughter Antonia.

1300    Fall of Acre, last Christian stronghold in the Holy Land (*Inf.* 27.89).

22 February: Pope Boniface VIII proclaims Jubilee Year (proclamation of a centenary indulgence for pilgrims to Rome).

1 May: Brawl erupts between White Guelfs, led by the Cerchi, and Black Guelfs, led by Corso Donati, in Piazza of Santa Trinita (*Inf.* 6.64–65).

7 May: Ambassador to San Gimignano on behalf of Guelfs.

June: Signs warrant sending Guido Cavalcanti into exile.

15 June–15 August: Election to Council of Priors, Florence's six-member executive board.

23 June: Another outbreak of hostilities between Florentine factions; 15 Blacks and Whites (Cavalcanti among the latter) banished by priors.

August: Death of Guido Cavalcanti (*Inf.* 10.68).

1301    1 April–15 September: Once again member of Council of the Hundred.

19 June: Only member of Council of the Hundred to vote against a proposal to furnish Pope Boniface VIII with 100 soldiers to fight the Santafiora in the Maremma.

October: Florentine embassy to Pope Boniface VIII, probably including Dante; Dante detained when pope sends most of the group back to Florence.

1 November: Charles of Valois and banished Black Guelfs enter Florence; White Guelfs fall from power.

1301–1310    Death of Arnolfo di Cambio.

1302    Pope Boniface VIII issues bull *Unam sanctam,* claiming supreme universal power in both spiritual and temporal spheres.

**27 January: Expelled from Florence for two years and fined 5,000 florins.**

February: Hostility of Boniface VIII and Charles of Valois reawakened by meeting in Gargonza of exiled Whites and Ghibellines.

**In Gargonza with exiled White Guelfs.**

**10 March: Dante's sentence—along with that of 14 other exiles—increased to death by being burned alive, in the event of return to Florence.**

May: Florentine Blacks and Lucchesi capture Serravalle from Whites of Pistoia.

**8 June: Meeting with exiled White Guelfs in the Mugello at San Godenzo to plan war against Blacks in the city; initial successes; military alliance in disarray by summer.**

July: Florentine Whites lose Castello of Piantravigne in the Valdarno due to treachery of Carlino de' Pazzi, who accepts bribe from Blacks (*Inf.* 32.52–69).

**Autumn: In Forlì as guest of Scarpetta degli Ordelaffi.**

(ca.) Death of Cimabue.

|       |       |
|-------|-------|
| 1303  | Repeated defeats of White Guelf–Ghibelline alliance in the Mugello. |

Fulcieri da Calboli becomes *Podestà* of Florence (*Purg.* 14.58–66).

7 September–October: Pope Boniface VIII captured at Anagni by Guillaume de Nogaret (Philip IV's advisor) and Ciarra Colonna (*Purg.* 20.86–90).

11 or 12 October: Death of Boniface VIII.

22 October: Election of Benedict XI as pope.

|           |       |
|-----------|-------|
| 1303–1304 | **May 1303–March 1304: In Verona as guest of Bartolomeo della Scala (*Par.* 17.70–72).** |

**Writes *De vulgari eloquentia* (left incomplete).**

|       |       |
|-------|-------|
| 1304  | January–April: Cardinal Niccolò da Prato enlisted by Benedict XI to act as peacemaker in Florence and to negotiate reconciliation between Black Guelfs and exiled Whites. |

**Still active as leader of exiled White Guelfs.**

**April: Leaves Verona with hope of helping Whites reenter Florence.**

April–August: In Arezzo, advises exiled Whites, then separates to make "a party unto [him]self" (*Par.* 17.69).

May–June: Writes *Epistola* 2 lamenting death of Alessandro da Romena, head of White Guelfs.

June: Blacks set fire that destroys 1,700 homes in center of Florence.

7 July: Death of Benedict XI.

20 July: Allied White Guelfs and Ghibellines suffer disastrous defeat at La Lastra outside Florence (Dante not present).

Birth of Petrarch.

| | |
|---|---|
| 1304–1305 | **Meets Giotto in Padua (Purg. 11).** |
| 1304–1306 | **In Treviso, as guest of Gherardo da Camino (*Purg.* 16.124), Dante in exile: Venice, Padua, and vicinity.** |
| 1304–1307 | **Writes *Convivio* (left unfinished).** |
| 1304–1309 | **Writes *Inferno*.** |
| 1305 | 5 June: Election of Clement V as pope. |
| | (ca.) Ubertino da Casale writes *Arbor Vitae Cruxifixae.* |
| 1305–1306 | Giotto's frescoes at Arena, or Scrovegni Chapel, Padua. |
| 1305–1378 | Clement V transfers papal see to Avignon (*Purg.* 32.158–160). |
| 1306 | Moroello Malaspina, leader of Black Guelfs of Lucca, defeats White Guelfs of Pistoia (*Inf.* 24.145–150). |
| 1306–1307 | **Autumn 1306–1307: In Lunigiana as guest of Moroello Malaspina.** |
| 1307 | **In the Casentino as guest of Guido Salvatico and Guido di Battifole.** |
| 1308 | 1 May: Assassination of Albert of Habsburg; election of Henry VII, count of Luxembourg, as emperor. |
| 1308–1309 | **Early 1308–March 1309: In Lucca (possibly with wife and children), befriended by "Gentucca" (*Purg.* 24.37); intense work on *Inferno*.** |
| 1308–1312 | **Writes *Purgatorio*.** |
| 1309 | March: Florentine exiles banished from Lucca. |
| | Death of Charles II of Anjou; accession of King Robert. |
| 1309–1310 | **In Paris (according to Villani, Boccaccio, Buti, and other early authorities).** |

| | |
|---|---|
| 1310 | Writes *Epistola* 5 exhorting Italy to receive Henry VII as emperor. |
| 1310–1311 | October 1310–January 1311: In Turin, Asti, Vercelli, and Milan accompanying Henry VII. |
| 1310–1313 | Henry VII of Luxembourg in Italy. |
| 1311 | January–late year: In the Casentino again as guest of Guido di Battifolle; works on *Purgatorio*. |
| | 6 January: Coronation of Henry VII as Holy Roman Emperor in Milan. |
| | 31 March: Writes *Epistola* 6 criticizing Florence's refusal to accept Henry VII as emperor. |
| | 17 April: Writes *Epistola* 7 to Henry VII exhorting him to enter Florence. |
| | April–May: Writes *Epistolae* 8, 9, and 10 congratulating Henry VII's wife on her husband's campaign (written for Guido di Battifolle's wife, Gherardesca). |
| | September: Dante's sons excluded from amnesty offered by Florentine government to White Guelf exiles. |
| 1312 | 29 June: Henry VII crowned emperor in Rome. |
| | Council of Vienne: Clement V suppresses Order of the Knights Templar. |
| 1312–1318 | May 1312–1318: In Verona as guest of Cangrande della Scala. |
| 1313 | Denounces "most wicked Florentines" in a Latin epistle (Ep. 7); condemns Clement V for simony and political treachery (*Inf.* 19.82–87, *Par.* 30.133–148). |
| | June: Uguccione della Faggiuola (Ghibelline Lord of Pisa) takes control of Lucca. |
| | 24 August: Death of Henry VII. |
| | Birth of Giovanni Boccaccio. |
| | Birth of Cola di Rienzo. |
| | (ca.) Giotto created *Navicella* mosaic in Rome. |
| 1314 | Pope Clement V reasserts papal rights over the Holy Roman Empire. |
| | 20 April: Death of Clement V. |
| | May: Writes *Epistola* 11 to Italian cardinals urging them to elect an Italian pope and end papacy's exile in Avignon. |

Albertino Mussato writes *Ecerinis* ("Ezzelino"), a Latin tragedy.

1314–1315    *Inferno* and *Purgatorio* in circulation.

1315          19 May: Florence, under severe threat from Ghibelline leader Uguccione della Faggiuola, offers exiles possibility of returning to city, upon payment of reduced fine and public penance.

             **Summer: Writes *Epistola* 12 to a friend, announcing his rejection of Florence's conditions for amnesty and return; refuses to accept any kind of "dishonor."**

             **15 October: Robert of Anjou's vicar in Tuscany condemns Dante and his sons to death by beheading.**

             24 August: Ghibellines, led by Uguccione della Faggiuola, defeat Guelfs at Battle of Montecatini.

             Simone Martini painted *Maestà* for town hall in Siena.

1316          April: Uguccione della Faggiuola expelled from Pisa and Lucca; succeeded by Castruccio Castracani in Lucca.

             Election of John XXII as pope.

1316–1321    Writes *Paradiso*.

             **Writes explanatory *Epistola* 13 dedicating *Paradiso* to Cangrande.**

1316–1317    Writes *Monarchia*.

1318–1321    **Early 1318–September 1321: In Ravenna as guest of Guido Novello da Polenta; children Pietro, Jacopo, and Antonia join him.**

1319–1320    Exchanges *Egloge* (*Eclogues*) with Giovanni del Virgilio.

1320          **20 January: Delivers *Quaestio de aqua et terra*, public lecture on the earth's dry land and seas, to learned audience in Verona.**

1321          **August–September: Mission as ambassador to Venice on behalf of Ravenna; contracts malarial fever on return.**

             **Night between 13–14 September: Death in Ravenna; buried in church of San Pier Maggiore (now San Francesco).**

             Founding of University of Florence.

             (ca.) Giotto began painting frescoes in Bardi and Peruzzi chapels in Santa Croce.

# Acknowledgments

We enjoyed writing this book immensely. We'd like to thank our agent, Scott Mendel, for his advice and support in planning and writing. We also would like to express our appreciation to our dynamic editor, Karen Wolny, and all the staff at Palgrave Macmillan involved in this project, especially Lauren Lo Pinto, Alan Bradshaw, Katherine Haigler, Lauren Dwyer, and Christine Catarino. It has been a pleasure working with such a professional and enthusiastic team of collaborators.

We are greatly indebted to Paul Barolsky for reading an earlier version of the manuscript with his characteristic combination of acumen and generosity.

Since Gustave Doré did not provide titles for his engravings of the *Inferno,* we have added provisional captions to facilitate the identification of the subject matter.

We are grateful to Princeton University Press for granting us permission to reproduce quotations from Dante, *The Divine Comedy: Inferno—2 Vols.* Translated by Charles Singleton © 1970 Princeton University Press, 1998, renewed PUP. Printed by permission of Princeton University Press.

Lastly, Deborah Parker would like to thank all the students who have taken Dante courses with her for the last 25 years. Their enthusiasm for Dante's works has been one of the highlights of more than two decades of teaching.

# Notes

## CHAPTER 2

1. Minos, judge of the damned, Cerberus, the monstrous three-headed dog that assails the gluttons, and Plutus, the wolf-like monster that presides over the avaricious and prodigal, all try (and fail) to stop Dante and Virgil. Dante adapts all these entities from classical literature. Some, like Cerberus and Charon, are commonplaces in classical treatments of the underworld.

## CHAPTER 3

1. *Inferno* 16 has links with cantos 6, 10, and 15, which also concern Florentine politics. There are parallels between 10 and 16 first: Farinata, Tegghiaio, Jacopo Rusticucci, and Guido Guerra are all from the same generation, the one just before Dante's. Each encounter begins with an elaborate recognition scene. Farinata recognized that Dante was a fellow Tuscan from his Florentine accent. The three sodomites perceived that Dante is Florentine from his clothing: "Stop, you who by your clothing seem to be / someone who comes from our indecent country" (*Inf.* 16.8–9). Dante, we might imagine, was wearing a long cassock and sleeveless tunic, just as illuminators typically depicted him in early manuscript illustrations. As in his encounter with Brunetto, Dante treats these men with courtesy—as Virgil instructs him to do—"Now wait: to these one must show courtesy." Haste is more appropriate to Dante—that is, haste to meet these souls—than to the three sodomites who run alongside him. There are also notable parallels with Dante's meeting with Brunetto Latini, the most obvious being the sin itself. As in the previous canto, Dante's barely alludes to the sin of homosexuality. We see an implicit contrast established between the good civic deeds of these men and what church doctrine held to be their private vices. The presentation juxtaposes a stern, implacable moral judgment with deep personal respect for their civic activities. These sinners embody admirable social and political values, yet they were also unrepentant

sodomites. Even at its best, humanity seems beset by torments and contradictions.

## CHAPTER 4

1. Dante also addresses the authority of the two rulers in his treatise *Monarchia* (*Monarchy,* ca. 1317). In Book 3, Dante outlines the relationship that he believes should exist between the governing powers, the Roman pontiff and the Roman emperor:

   "But the truth concerning this last question should not be taken so literally as to mean that the Roman Prince is not in some sense subject to the Roman Pontiff, since this earthly happiness is in some sense ordered towards immortal happiness. Let Caesar therefore show that reverence towards Peter which a firstborn son should show his father, so that, illumined by the light of paternal grace, he may the more effectively light up the world, over which he has been placed by Him alone, who is ruler over all things spiritual and temporal."

   Dante presents the two leaders as two luminaries, each having his own sphere of influence. Since earthly happiness is ultimately ordered toward immortal happiness, the Roman prince or emperor should show reverence to Peter, that is, the pope (all popes are successors to St. Peter, the first pope) as a son reveres his father. Dante wrote the *Monarchia* to address, at least in part, the unprecedented expansion of papal authority taking place in his time.

2. Some of this background information is derived from the entry on Boniface VIII in *The Dante Encyclopedia,* ed. Richard Lansing (New York: Garland Publishing, 2000), 122–124, and Brenda Bolton, "Papal Italy," in *Italy in the Central Middle Ages: 1100–1300* (New York: Oxford University Press, 2004), 82–103.

3. Bolton, "Papal Italy," 82.

4. Pietro Alighieri cited in Charles S. Singleton, *The Divine Comedy: Inferno Commentary* (Princeton, NJ: Princeton University Press, 1970), 59.

5. Dante alludes to the sins against nature in *Inferno* 11 by mentioning two cities, Sodom and Cahors. In the Bible, God destroyed Sodom as a den of iniquity. Cahors in France was notorious for the practice of usury.

6. *The Divine Comedy of Dante Alighieri, Inferno,* trans. Robert M. Durling and Ronald L. Martinez (New York: Oxford University Press, 1997), 356.

7. Line 66 suggests that the punishment was also inspired by a historical punishment. Emperor Frederick II punished traitors to his court by forcing them to don coats of lead. He then ordered them placed over a cauldron. The fire under the cauldron caused the lead to melt, and the traitor's skin fell off in shreds. So heavy are these infernal capes, those devised by Frederick seem like straw.

8. The punishment of the simonists might also have been inspired by the way in which the apostle Peter was martyred. Peter asked to be crucified

upside-down as he deemed himself unworthy to be crucified in the same way as Jesus. Peter is an important figure in the canto even though he is invoked only a couple of times. His name Peter derives from the Greek *petros,* "rock." Jesus told Peter, ""I also say to *you* that *you* are Peter, and upon this rock *I* will build My church" (Matthew 16:18).

9. Elsewhere in the poem, Dante condemns Clement V for his role in the destruction of the Templars (*Purg.* 20.91–93), the removal of the papal see to Avignon (*Purg.* 32.157–160); and his betrayal of Henry VII (*Par.* 30.142–148).

10. Singleton, *Inferno Commentary,* 474.

11. Ibid., 486.

## CHAPTER 5

1. To view Hensman's map, see http://www.worldofdante.org/dantemap _detail.html.

2. T. S. Eliot, *The Sacred Wood* (New York: Alfred A. Knopf, 1921), p. 162, emphasis in original.

3. T. S. Eliot, *Dante* (London: Faber & Faber, 1929), pp. 22, 23; emphasis in original.

4. At the end of *Inferno 25,* Dante mentions Gaville, a Tuscan village in the upper Valdarno. Home of Francesco de' Cavalcanti, it was almost completely decimated by the Cavalcanti after one of their kinsman was killed there. Gaville, then, is the site of another atrocious crime.

## CHAPTER 7

1. Matthew Pearl, *The Dante Club* (New York: Random House, 2003), p. 8.

2. Sandow Birk and Marcus Sanders, *Dante's Inferno* (San Franscisco: Chronicle Books LLC, 2004).

## CHAPTER 8

1. "Inferno is not an activist book," *The Independent,* 14 May 2013, http://www.independent.co.uk/arts-entertainment/books/news/dan -brown-inferno-is-is-not-an-activist-book-i-dont-have-a-solution-to -overpopulation-8615276.html.

# *Bibliography*

## PRIMARY SOURCES CITED

Alighieri, Dante. *Dante. The Inferno, Purgatorio, Paradiso.* Translated by Robert Hollander and Jean Hollander. New York: Doubleday, 2000-2007.

——. *The Divine Comedy.* Translated with a commentary by Charles S. Singleton. Princeton, NJ: Princeton University Press, 1970.

——. *The Divine Comedy of Dante Alighieri. Inferno.* Translated by Robert M. Durling and Ronald L. Martinez. New York: Oxford University Press, 1996.

——. *La Vita Nuova* [Poems of Youth]. Trans. Barbara Reynolds. New York: Penguin Books, 1969, rpt. 1980.

Birk, Sandow, and Marcus Sanders. *Dante's Inferno.* San Francisco, Chronicle Books, 2004.

Brown, Dan. *Inferno.* New York: Doubleday, 2013.

Pearl, Matthew. *The Dante Club.* New York: Random House, 2003.

Pound, Ezra. *The Cantos of Ezra Pound.* New York: New Directions, 1996.

## FOR READERS SEEKING MORE INFORMATION ON DANTE, WE SUGGEST THE FOLLOWING WORKS AND WEB SITES.

### Books and Articles

Auerbach, Erich. *Dante: Poet of the Secular World.* Translated by Ralph Manheim. Chicago: University of Chicago Press, 1961, rpt. 1974

Bolton, Brenda. "Papal Italy," in *Italy in the Central Middle Ages: 1100–1300 (Short Oxford History of Italy).* New York: Oxford University Press, 2004, 82–103.

Eliot, T. S. *The Complete Poems and Plays, 1909-1950.* New York: Harcourt, Brace & World, Inc., 1971.

Eliot, T. S. *Dante.* London: Faber & Faber, 1929.

Havely, Nick. *Dante.* Malden, MA: Blackwell, 2007.

Parker, Deborah. "Illuminating Botticelli's Chart of Hell," *Modern Language Notes: Italian Issue* 128 (2013): 83–102.

Raffa, Guy P. *The Complete Danteworlds: A Reader's Guide to the Divine Comedy.* Chicago: University of Chicago Press, 2009.

Taylor, Charles H., and Patricia Finley, eds. *Images of the Journey in Dante's Divine Comedy.* New Haven, CT: Yale University Press, 2007.

### Online Resources

Princeton Dante Project: http://etcweb.princeton.edu/dante/index.html

University of Texas at Austin: Welcome to Danteworlds: http://danteworlds.laits.utexas.edu/

The World of Dante: http://www.worldofdante.org

# Index